MATLAB Differential Equations

César Pérez López

MATLAB Differential Equations

ISBN-13 (pbk): 978-1-4842-0311-8

ISBN-13 (electronic): 978-1-4842-0310-1

Publisher: Heinz Weinheimer
Lead Editor: Dominic Shakeshaft
Editorial Board: Steve Anglin, Mark Beckner, Ewan Buckingham, Gary Cornell, Louise Corrigan, Jim DeWolf, Jonathan Gennick, Jonathan Hassell, Robert Hutchinson, Michelle Lowman, James Markham, Matthew Moodie, Jeff Olson, Jeffrey Pepper, Douglas Pundick, Ben Renow-Clarke, Dominic Shakeshaft, Gwenan Spearing, Matt Wade, Steve Weiss
Coordinating Editor: Melissa Maldonado
Copy Editor: Barnaby Sheppard
Compositor: SPi Global
Indexer: SPi Global
Artist: SPi Global
Cover Designer: Anna Ishchenko

Distributed to the book trade worldwide by Springer Science+Business Media New York, 233 Spring Street, 6th Floor, New York, NY 10013. Phone 1-800-SPRINGER, fax (201) 348-4505, e-mail orders-ny@springer-sbm.com, or visit www.springeronline.com. Apress Media, LLC is a California LLC and the sole member (owner) is Springer Science + Business Media Finance Inc (SSBM Finance Inc). SSBM Finance Inc is a **Delaware** corporation.

For information on translations, please e-mail rights@apress.com, or visit www.apress.com.

Apress and friends of ED books may be purchased in bulk for academic, corporate, or promotional use. eBook versions and licenses are also available for most titles. For more information, reference our Special Bulk Sales–eBook Licensing web page at www.apress.com/bulk-sales.

Any source code or other supplementary material referenced by the author in this text is available to readers at www.apress.com. For detailed information about how to locate your book's source code, go to www.apress.com/source-code/.

Contents at a Glance

Contents

About the Author

César Pérez López is a Professor at the Department of Statistics and Operations Research at the University of Madrid. César is also a Mathematician and Economist at the National Statistics Institute (INE) in Madrid, a body which belongs to the Superior Systems and Information Technology Department of the Spanish Government. César also currently works at the Institute for Fiscal Studies in Madrid.

Coming Soon

- *MATLAB Programming for Numerical Analysis,* 978-1-4842-0296-8
- *MATLAB Control Systems Engineering,* 978-1-4842-0290-6
- *MATLAB Linear Algebra,* 978-1-4842-0323-1
- *MATLAB Differential and Integral Calculus,* 978-1-4842-0305-7
- *MATLAB Matrix Algebra,* 978-1-4842-0308-8

■ ■ ■

CHAPTER 1

Introducing MATLAB and the MATLAB Working Environment

Introduction

MATLAB is a platform for scientific calculation and high-level programming which uses an interactive environment that allows you to conduct complex calculation tasks more efficiently than with traditional languages, such as C, C++ and FORTRAN. It is the one of the most popular platforms currently used in the sciences and engineering.

MATLAB is an interactive high-level technical computing environment for algorithm development, data visualization, data analysis and numerical analysis. MATLAB is suitable for solving problems involving technical calculations using optimized algorithms that are incorporated into easy to use commands.

It is possible to use MATLAB for a wide range of applications, including calculus, algebra, statistics, econometrics, quality control, time series, signal and image processing, communications, control system design, testing and measuring systems, financial modeling, computational biology, etc. The complementary toolsets, called *toolboxes* (collections of MATLAB functions for special purposes, which are available separately), extend the MATLAB environment, allowing you to solve special problems in different areas of application.

In addition, MATLAB contains a number of functions which allow you to document and share your work. It is possible to integrate MATLAB code with other languages and applications, and to distribute algorithms and applications that are developed using MATLAB.

The following are the most important features of MATLAB:

- It is a high-level language for technical calculation

- It offers a development environment for managing code, files and data

- It features interactive tools for exploration, design and iterative solving

- It supports mathematical functions for linear algebra, statistics, Fourier analysis, filtering, optimization, and numerical integration

- It can produce high quality two-dimensional and three-dimensional graphics to aid data visualization

- It includes tools to create custom graphical user interfaces

- It can be integrated with external languages, such as C/C++, FORTRAN, Java, COM, and Microsoft Excel

The MATLAB development environment allows you to develop algorithms, analyze data, display data files and manage projects in interactive mode (see Figure 1-1).

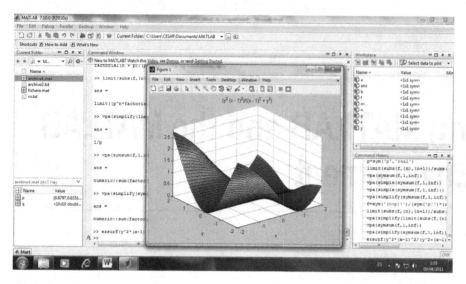

Figure 1-1.

Developing Algorithms and Applications

MATLAB provides a high-level programming language and development tools which enable you to quickly develop and analyze algorithms and applications.

The MATLAB language includes vector and matrix operations that are fundamental to solving scientific and engineering problems. This streamlines both development and execution.

With the MATLAB language, it is possible to program and develop algorithms faster than with traditional languages because it is no longer necessary to perform low level administrative tasks, such as declaring variables, specifying data types and allocating memory. In many cases, MATLAB eliminates the need for 'for' loops. As a result, a line of MATLAB code usually replaces several lines of C or C++ code.

At the same time, MATLAB offers all the features of traditional programming languages, including arithmetic operators, control flow, data structures, data types, object-oriented programming (OOP) and debugging.

Figure 1-2 shows a communication modulation algorithm that generates 1024 random bits, performs the modulation, adds complex Gaussian noise and graphically represents the result, all in just nine lines of MATLAB code.

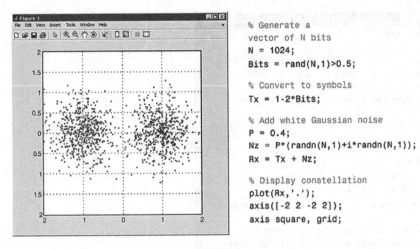

```
% Generate a
vector of N bits
N = 1024;
Bits = rand(N,1)>0.5;

% Convert to symbols
Tx = 1-2*Bits;

% Add white Gaussian noise
P = 0.4;
Nz = P*(randn(N,1)+i*randn(N,1));
Rx = Tx + Nz;

% Display constellation
plot(Rx,'.');
axis([-2 2 -2 2]);
axis square, grid;
```

Figure 1-2.

MATLAB enables you to execute commands or groups of commands one at a time, without compiling or linking, and to repeat the execution to achieve the optimal solution.

To quickly execute complex vector and matrix calculations, MATLAB uses libraries optimized for the processor. For general scalar calculations, MATLAB generates instructions in machine code using JIT (*Just-In-Time*) technology. Thanks to this technology, which is available for most platforms, the execution speeds are much faster than for traditional programming languages.

MATLAB includes *development tools*, which help efficiently implement algorithms. Some of these tools are listed below:

- **MATLAB Editor** – used for editing functions and standard debugging, for example setting breakpoints and running step-by-step simulations

- **M-Lint Code Checker** - analyzes the code and recommends changes to improve performance and maintenance (see Figure 1-3)

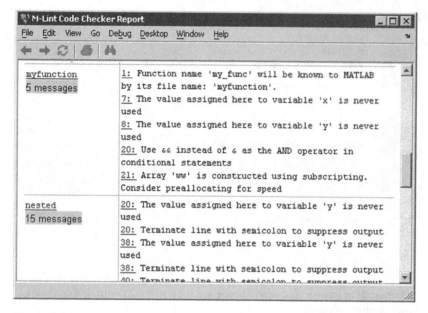

Figure 1-3.

- **MATLAB Profiler** - records the time taken to execute each line of code

- **Directory Reports** - scans all files in a directory and creates reports about the efficiency of the code, differences between files, dependencies of files and code coverage

You can also use the interactive tool GUIDE (*Graphical User Interface Development Environment*) to design and edit user interfaces. This tool allows you to include pick lists, drop-down menus, push buttons, radio buttons and sliders, as well as MATLAB diagrams and ActiveX controls. You can also create graphical user interfaces by means of programming using MATLAB functions.

Figure 1-4 shows a completed wavelet analysis tool (below) which has been created using the user interface GUIDE (above).

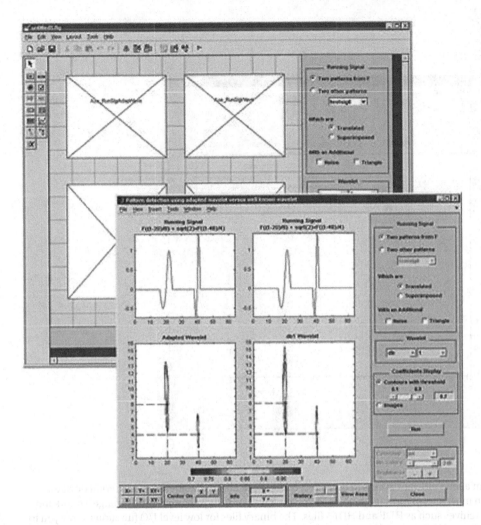

Figure 1-4.

Data Access and Analysis

MATLAB supports the entire process of data analysis, from the acquisition of data from external devices and databases, pre-processing, visualization and numerical analysis, up to the production of results in presentation quality.

MATLAB provides interactive tools and command line operations for data analysis, which include: sections of data, scaling and averaging, interpolation, thresholding and smoothing, correlation, Fourier analysis and filtering, searching for one-dimensional peaks and zeros, basic statistics and curve fitting, matrix analysis, etc.

The diagram in Figure 1-5 shows a curve that has been fitted to atmospheric pressure differences averaged between Easter Island and Darwin in Australia.

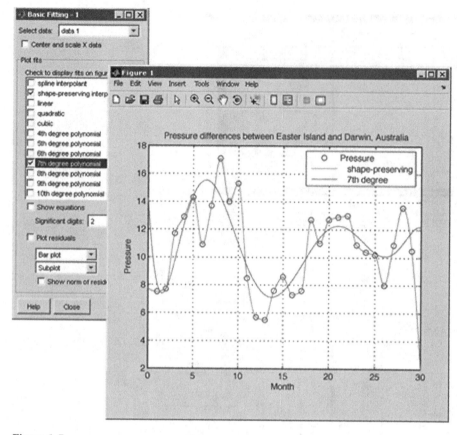

Figure 1-5.

The MATLAB platform allows efficient access to data files, other applications, databases and external devices. You can read data stored in most known formats, such as Microsoft Excel, ASCII text files or binary image, sound and video files, and scientific archives such as HDF and HDF5 files. The binary files for low level I/O functions allow you to work with data files in any format. Additional features allow you to view Web pages and XML data.

It is possible to call other applications and languages, such as C, C++, COM, DLLs, Java, FORTRAN, and Microsoft Excel objects, and access FTP sites and Web services. Using the Database Toolbox, you can even access ODBC/JDBC databases.

Data Visualization

All graphics functions necessary to visualize scientific and engineering data are available in MATLAB. This includes tools for two- and three-dimensional diagrams, three-dimensional volume visualization, tools to create diagrams interactively, and the ability to export using the most popular graphic formats. It is possible to customize diagrams, adding multiple axes, changing the colors of lines and markers, adding annotations, LaTeX equations and legends and plotting paths.

Various two-dimensional graphical representations of vector data can be created, including:

- Line, area, bar and sector diagrams

- Direction and velocity diagrams

- Histograms
- Polygons and surfaces
- Dispersion bubble diagrams
- Animations

Figure 1-6 shows linear plots of the results of several emission tests of a motor, with a curve fitted to the data.

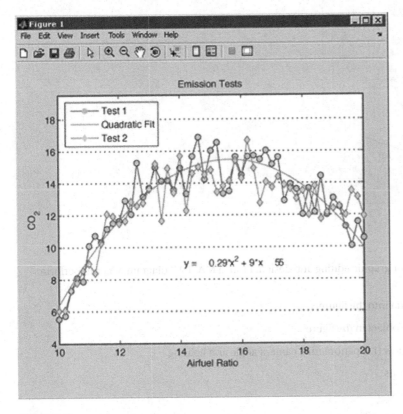

Figure 1-6.

MATLAB also provides functions for displaying two-dimensional arrays, three-dimensional scalar data and three-dimensional vector data. It is possible to use these functions to visualize and understand large amounts of complex multi-dimensional data. It is also possible to define the characteristics of the diagrams, such as the orientation of the camera, perspective, lighting, light source and transparency. Three-dimensional diagramming features include:

- Surface, contour and mesh plots
- Space curves
- Cone, phase, flow and isosurface diagrams

Figure 1-7 shows a three-dimensional diagram of an isosurface that reveals the geodesic structure of a fullerene carbon-60 molecule.

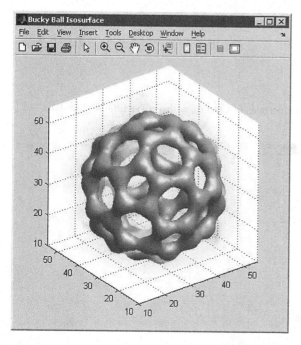

Figure 1-7.

MATLAB includes interactive tools for graphic editing and design. From a MATLAB diagram, you can perform any of the following tasks:

- Drag and drop new sets of data into the figure

- Change the properties of any object in the figure

- Change the zoom, rotation, view (i.e. panoramic), camera angle and lighting

- Add data labels and annotations

- Draw shapes

- Generate an M-file for reuse with different data

Figure 1-8 shows a collection of graphics which have been created interactively by dragging data sets onto the diagram window, making new subdiagrams, changing properties such as colors and fonts, and adding annotations.

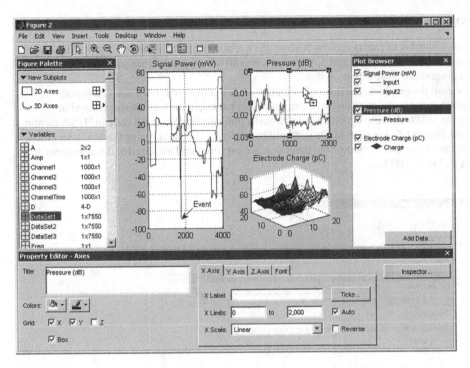

Figure 1-8.

MATLAB is compatible with all the well-known data file and graphics formats, such as GIF, JPEG, BMP, EPS, TIFF, PNG, HDF, AVI, and PCX. As a result, it is possible to export MATLAB diagrams to other applications, such as Microsoft Word and Microsoft Powerpoint, or desktop publishing software. Before exporting, you can create and apply style templates that contain all the design details, fonts, line thickness, etc., necessary to comply with the publication specifications.

Numerical Calculation

MATLAB contains mathematical, statistical, and engineering functions that support most of the operations carried out in those fields. These functions, developed by math experts, are the foundation of the MATLAB language. To cite some examples, MATLAB implements mathematical functions and data analysis in the following areas:

- Manipulation of matrices and linear algebra
- Polynomials and interpolation
- Fourier analysis and filters
- Statistics and data analysis
- Optimization and numerical integration
- Ordinary differential equations (ODEs)
- Partial differential equations (PDEs)
- Sparse matrix operations

9

Publication of Results and Distribution of Applications

In addition, MATLAB contains a number of functions which allow you to document and share your work. You can integrate your MATLAB code with other languages and applications, and distribute your algorithms and MATLAB applications as autonomous programs or software modules.

MATLAB allows you to export the results in the form of a diagram or as a complete report. You can export diagrams to all popular graphics formats and then import them into other packages such as Microsoft Word or Microsoft PowerPoint. Using the MATLAB Editor, you can automatically publish your MATLAB code in HTML format, Word, LaTeX, etc. For example, Figure 1-9 shows an M-file (left) published in HTML (right) using the MATLAB Editor. The results, which are sent to the Command Window or to diagrams, are captured and included in the document and the comments become titles and text in HTML.

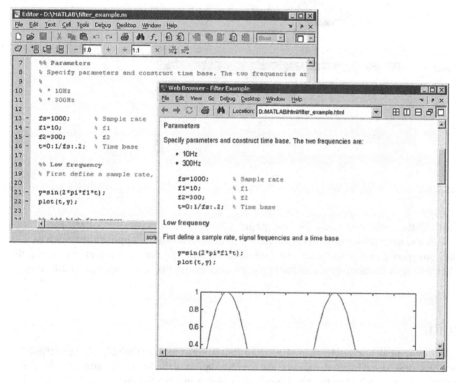

Figure 1-9.

It is possible to create more complex reports, such as mock executions and various parameter tests, using MATLAB Report Generator (available separately).

MATLAB provides functions enabling you to integrate your MATLAB applications with C and C++ code, FORTRAN code, COM objects, and Java code. You can call DLLs and Java classes and ActiveX controls. Using the MATLAB engine library, you can also call MATLAB from C, C++, or FORTRAN code.

You can create algorithms in MATLAB and distribute them to other users of MATLAB. Using the MATLAB Compiler (available separately), algorithms can be distributed, either as standalone applications or as software modules included in a project, to users who do not have MATLAB. Additional products are able to turn algorithms into a software module that can be called from COM or Microsoft Excel.

The MATLAB working environment

Figure 1-10 shows the primary workspace of the MATLAB environment. This is the screen in which you enter your MATLAB programs.

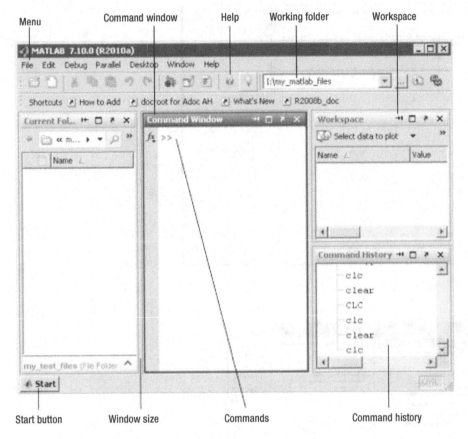

Figure 1-10.

The following table summarizes the components of the MATLAB environment.

Tool	Description
Command History	This allows you to see the commands entered during the session in the Command Window, as well as copy them and run them (lower right part of Figure 1-11)
Command Window	This is where you enter MATLAB commands (central part of Figure 1-11)
Workspace	This allows you to view the contents of the workspace (variables, etc.) (upper right part of Figure 1-11)
Help	This offers help and demos on MATLAB
Start button	This enables you to run tools and provides access to MATLAB documentation (Figure 1-12)

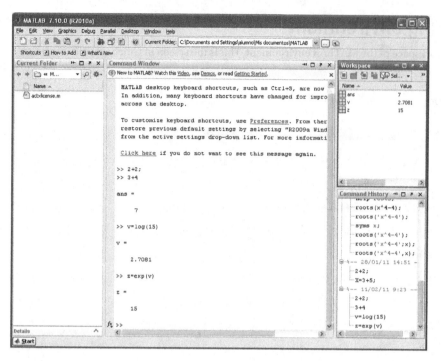

Figure 1-11.

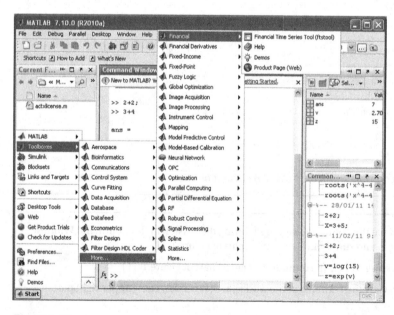

Figure 1-12.

MATLAB commands are written in the Command Window to the right of the user input prompt "»" and the response to the command will appear in the lines immediately below. After exiting from the response, the user input prompt will re-display, allowing you to input more entries (Figure 1-13).

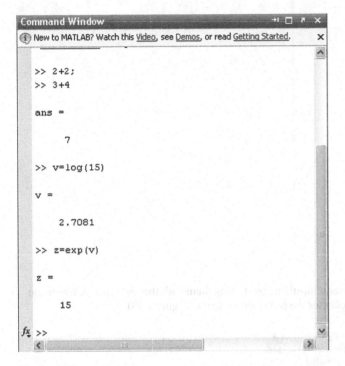

Figure 1-13.

When an input is given to MATLAB in the Command Window and the result is not assigned to a variable, the response returned will begin with the expression "***ans=***", as shown near the top of Figure 1-13. If the results are assigned to a variable, we can then use that variable as an argument for subsequent input. This is the case for the variable v in Figure 1-13, which is subsequently used as the input for an exponential.

To run a MATLAB command, simply type the command and press *Enter*. If at the end of the input we put a semicolon, the program runs the calculation and keeps it in memory (*Workspace*), but does not display the result on the screen (see the first entry in Figure 1-13). The input prompt "»" appears to indicate that you can enter a new command.

Like the C programming language, MATLAB is case sensitive; for example, $Sin(x)$ is not the same as $sin(x)$. The names of all built-in functions begin with a lowercase character. There should be no spaces in the names of commands, variables or functions. In other cases, spaces are ignored, and they can be used to make the input more readable. Multiple entries can be entered in the same command line by separating them with commas, pressing *Enter* at the end of the last entry (see Figure 1-14). If you use a semicolon at the end of one of the entries in the line, its corresponding output will not be displayed.

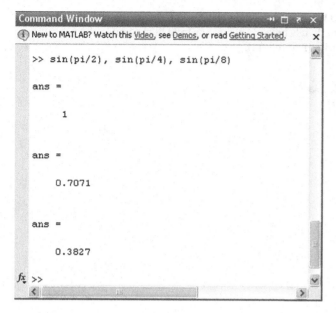

Figure 1-14.

Descriptive comments can be entered in a command input line by starting them with the "%" symbol. When you run the input, MATLAB ignores the comment and processes the rest of the code (see Figure 1-15).

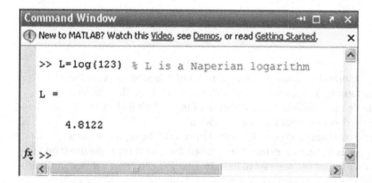

Figure 1-15.

To simplify the process of entering script to be evaluated by the MATLAB interpreter (via the Command Window prompt), you can use the arrow keys. For example, if you press the up arrow key once, you will recover the last entry you submitted. If you press the up key twice, you will recover the penultimate entry you submitted, and so on.

If you type a sequence of characters in the input area and then press the up arrow key, you will recover the last entry you submitted that begins with the specified string.

Commands entered during a MATLAB session are temporarily stored in the buffer (*Workspace*) until you end the session, at which time they can be permanently stored in a file or are permanently lost.

Below is a summary of the keys that can be used in MATLAB's input area (command line), together with their functions:

Up arrow (Ctrl-P)	Retrieves the previous entry.
Down arrow (Ctrl-N)	Retrieves the following entry.
Left arrow (Ctrl-B)	Moves the cursor one character to the left.
Right arrow (Ctrl-F)	Moves the cursor one character to the right.
CTRL-left arrow	Moves the cursor one word to the left.
CTRL-right arrow	Moves the cursor one word to the right.
Home (Ctrl-A)	Moves the cursor to the beginning of the line.
End (Ctrl-E)	Moves the cursor to the end of the current line.
Escape	Clears the command line.
Delete (Ctrl-D)	Deletes the character indicated by the cursor.
Backspace	Deletes the character to the left of the cursor.
CTRL-K	Deletes (kills) the current line.

The command *clc* clears the command window, but does not delete the contents of the work area (the contents remain in the memory).

Help in MATLAB

You can find help for MATLAB via the help button ⍰ in the tool bar or via the *Help* option in the menu bar. In addition, support can also be obtained via MATLAB commands. The command *help* provides general help on all MATLAB commands (see Figure 1-16). By clicking on any of them, you can get more specific help. For example, if you click on the command *graph2d*, you get support for two-dimensional graphics (see Figure 1-17).

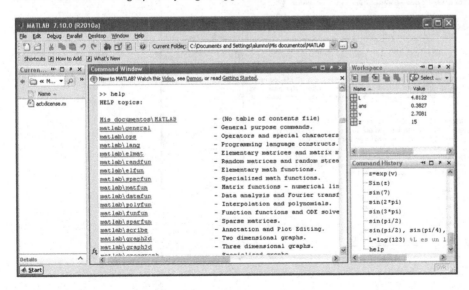

Figure 1-16.

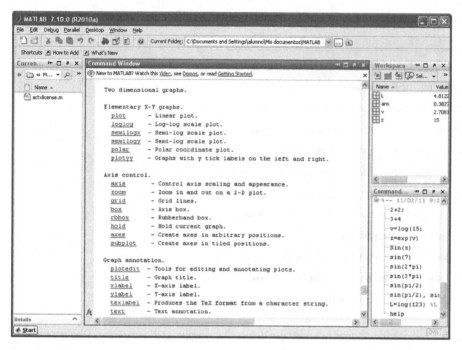

Figure 1-17.

You can ask for help about a specific command *command* (Figure 1-18) or on any topic *topic* (Figure 1-19) by using the command *help command* or *help topic*.

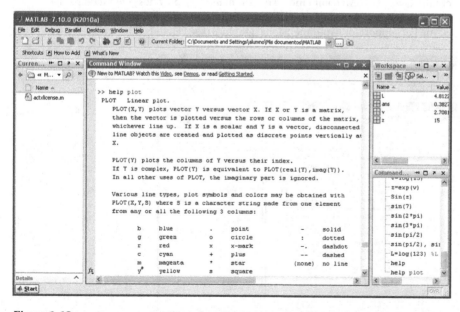

Figure 1-18.

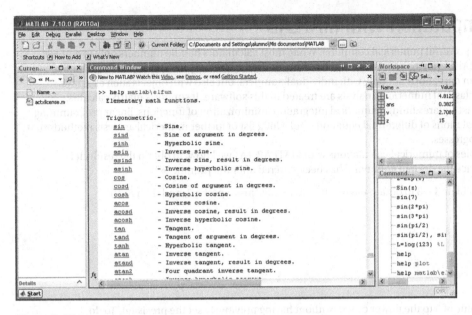

Figure 1-19.

The command *lookfor string* allows you to find all those MATLAB functions or commands that refer to or contain the string *string*. This command is very useful when there is no direct support for the specified string, or to view the help for all commands related to the given string. For example, if we want to find help for all commands that contain the sequence *inv*, we can use the command *lookfor inv* (Figure 1-20).

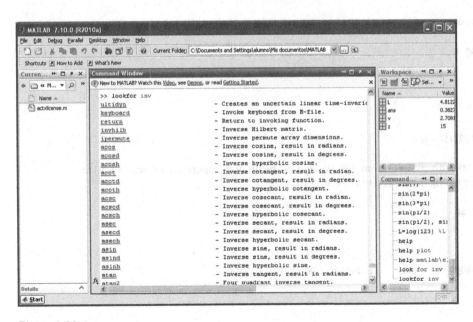

Figure 1-20.

Numerical Computation with MATLAB

You can use MATLAB as a powerful numerical computer. While most calculators handle numbers only to a preset degree of precision, MATLAB performs exact calculations to any desired degree of precision. In addition, unlike calculators, we can perform operations not only with individual numbers, but also with objects such as arrays.

Most of the topics of classical numerical analysis are treated in this software. It supports matrix calculus, statistics, interpolation, least squares fitting, numerical integration, minimization of functions, linear programming, numerical and algebraic solutions of differential equations and a long list of further numerical analysis methods that we'll meet as this book progresses.

Here are some examples of numerical calculations with MATLAB. (As we know, to obtain the results it is necessary to press *Enter* once the desired command has been entered after the prompt "»".)

1. We simply calculate 4 + 3 to obtain the result 7. To do this, just type 4 + 3, and then *Enter*.

    » 4 + 3

    ans =

    7

2. We find the value of 3 to the power of 100, without having previously set the precision. To do this we simply enter 3 ^ 100.

    » 3 ^ 100

    ans =

    5. 1538e + 047

3. We can use the command "format long e" to obtain results to 15 digits (floating-point).

    » format long e

    » 3^100

    ans =

    5.153775207320115e+047

4. We can also work with complex numbers. We find the result of the operation raising (2 + 3i) to the power 10 by typing the expression (2 + 3i) ^ 10.

    » (2 + 3i) ^ 10

    ans =

    -1 415249999999998e + 005 - 1. 456680000000000e + 005i

5. The previous result is also available in short format, using the "format short" command.

    » **format short**
    » **(2 + 3i)^10**

    ans =

    -1.4152e+005- 1.4567e+005i

6. We can calculate the value of the Bessel function J_0 at 11.5. To do this we type besselj(0,11.5).

    >> **besselj(0,11.5)**

    ans =

    -0.0677

Symbolic Calculations with MATLAB

MATLAB perfectly handles symbolic mathematical computations, manipulating and performing operations on formulae and algebraic expressions with ease. You can expand, factor and simplify polynomials and rational and trigonometric expressions, find algebraic solutions of polynomial equations and systems of equations, evaluate derivatives and integrals symbolically, find solutions of differential equations, manipulate powers, and investigate limits and many other features of algebraic series.

To perform these tasks, MATLAB first requires all the variables (or algebraic expressions) to be written between single quotes. When MATLAB receives a variable or expression in quotes, it is interpreted as symbolic.

Here are some examples of symbolic computations with MATLAB.

1. We can expand the following algebraic expression: ((x+1)(x+2)-(x+2)^2)^3.
    This is done by typing: expand('(x+1)(x+2)-(x+2)^2)^3'). The result will be another
    algebraic expression:

    » **syms x; expand(((x + 1) *(x + 2)-(x + 2) ^ 2) ^ 3)**

    ans =

    -x ^ 3-6 * x ^ 2-12 * x-8

2. We can factor the result of the calculation in the above example by typing:
    factor('((x + 1) *(x + 2)-(x + 2) ^ 2) ^ 3')

    » **syms x; factor(((x + 1)*(x + 2)-(x + 2)^2)^3)**

    ans =

    -(x+2)^3

3. We can find the indefinite integral of the function $(x \wedge 2) \sin(x) \wedge 2$ by typing:
    int('x ∧ 2 * sin(x) ∧ 2', 'x')

    ```
    » int('x^2*sin(x)^2', 'x')
    ```

    ans =

    x ∧ 2 *(-1/2 * cos(x) * sin(x) + 1/2 * x)-1/2 * x * cos(x) ∧ 2 + 1/4 * cos(x) * sin(x) + 1/4 * 1/x-3 * x ∧ 3

4. We can simplify the previous result:

    ```
    >> syms x; simplify(int(x^2*sin(x)^2, x))
    ```

    ans =

    sin(2*x)/8 -(x*cos(2*x))/4 -(x^2*sin(2*x))/4 + x^3/6

5. We can present the previous result using a more elegant mathematical notation:

    ```
    >> syms x; pretty(simplify(int(x^2*sin(x)^2, x)))
    ```

    ans =

    $$\frac{\sin(2\ x)}{8} - \frac{x\ \cos(2\ x)}{4} - \frac{x^2\ \sin(2\ x)}{4} + \frac{x^3}{6}$$

6. We can solve the equation $3ax-7 x \wedge 2 + x \wedge 3 = 0$ (where a is a parameter):

    ```
    » solve('3*a*x-7*x^2 + x^3 = 0', 'x')
    ```

    ans =

    [0]
    [7/2 + 1/2 *(49-12*a) ^(1/2)]
    [7/2-1/2 *(49-12*a) ^(1/2)]

On the other hand, MATLAB can use the Maple program libraries to work with symbolic math, and can thus extend its field of action. In this way, MATLAB can be used to work on such topics as differential forms, Euclidean geometry, projective geometry, statistics, etc.

At the same time, Maple can also benefit from MATLAB's powers of numerical calculation, which might be used, for example, in combination with the Maple libraries (combinatorics, optimization, number theory, etc.)

Graphics with MATLAB

MATLAB can generate two- and three-dimensional graphs, as well as contour and density plots. You can graphically represent data lists, controlling colors, shading and other graphics features. Animated graphics are also supported. Graphics produced by MATLAB are portable to other programs.

Some examples of MATLAB graphics are given below.

1. We can represent the function $x\sin(1/x)$ for x ranging between $-\pi/4$ and $\pi/4$, taking 300 equidistant points in the interval. See Figure 1-21.

```
» x = linspace(-pi/4,pi/4,300);
» y=x.*sin(1./x);
» plot(x,y)
```

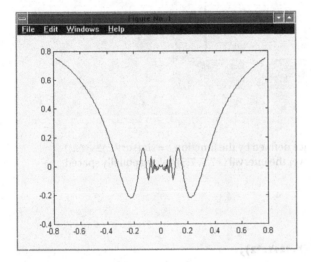

Figure 1-21.

2. We can give the above graph a title and label the axes, and we can add a grid. See Figure 1-22.

```
» x = linspace(-pi/4,pi/4,300);
» y=x.*sin(1./x);
» plot(x,y);
» grid;
» xlabel('Independent variable X');
» ylabel('Dependent variable Y');
» title('The function y=xsin(1/x)')
```

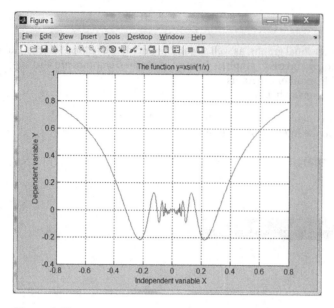

Figure 1-22.

3. We can generate a graph of the surface defined by the function $z = \sin(\text{sqrt}(x^2+y^2))$ /sqrt(x^2+y^2), where x and y vary over the interval (- 7.5, 7.5), taking equally spaced points 0.5 apart. See Figure 1-23.

```
» x =-7.5:. 5:7.5;
» y = x;
» [X, Y] = meshgrid(x,y);
» Z=sin(sqrt(X.^2+Y.^2))./sqrt(X.^2+Y.^2);
» surf(X, Y, Z)
```

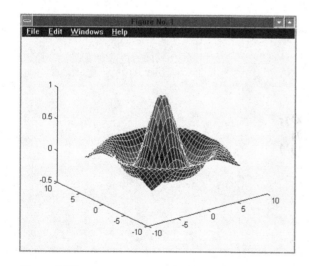

Figure 1-23.

These 3D graphics allow you to get a clear picture of figures in space, and are very helpful in visually identifying intersections between different bodies, and in generating all kinds of space curves, surfaces and volumes of revolution.

4. We can generate the three dimensional graph corresponding to the helix with parametric coordinates: $x = \sin(t)$, $y = \cos(t)$, $z = t$. See Figure 1-24.

```
» t=0:pi/50:10*pi;
» plot3(sin(t),cos(t),t)
```

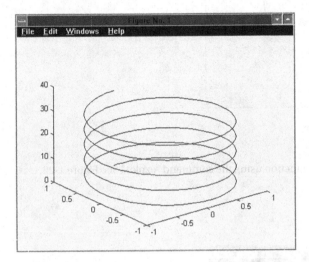

Figure 1-24.

5. We can represent a planar curve given by its polar coordinates r = cos(2t) * sin(2t) for *t* varying in the range between 0 and π by equally spaced points 0.01 apart. See Figure 1-25.

```
» t = 0:. 1:2 * pi;
» r = sin(2*t). * cos(2*t);
» polar(t,r)
```

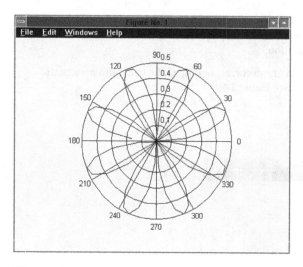

Figure 1-25.

6. We can make a graph of a symbolic function using the command "ezplot". See Figure 1-26.

```
» y ='x ^ 3 /(x^2-1)';
» ezplot(y,[-5,5])
```

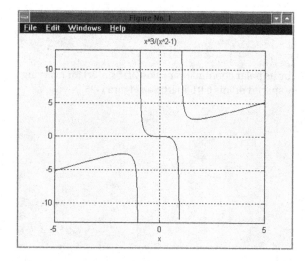

Figure 1-26.

We will go into these concepts in more detail in the chapter on graphics.

General Notation

As for any program, the best way to learn MATLAB is to use it. By practicing on examples you become familiar with the syntax and notation peculiar to MATLAB. Each example we give consists of the header with the user input prompt "»" followed by the MATLAB response on the next line. See Figure 1-27.

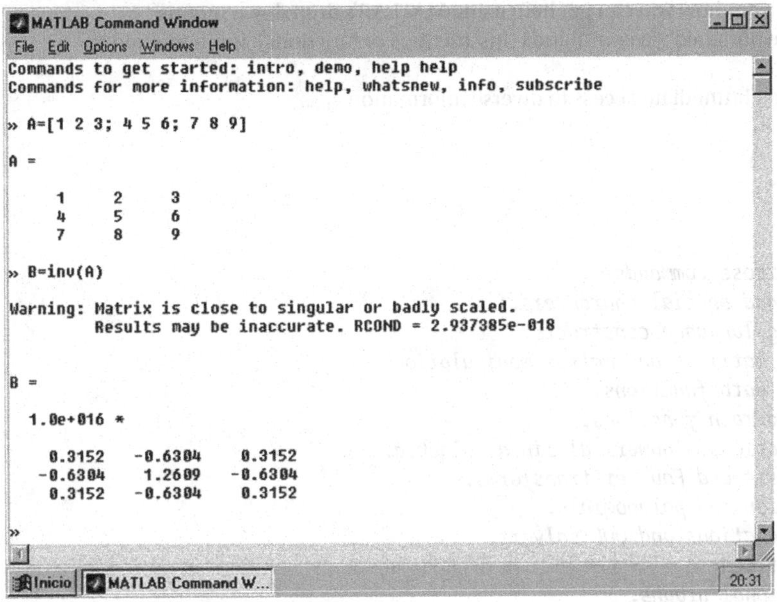

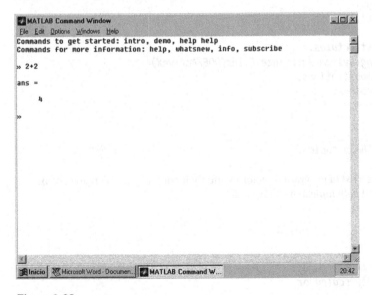

Figure 1-27.

At other times, depending on the type of entry (user input) given to MATLAB, the response is returned using the expression "ans =". See Figure 1-28.

Figure 1-28.

It is important to pay attention to the use of uppercase versus lowercase letters, parentheses versus square brackets, spaces and punctuation (particularly commas and semicolons).

Help with Commands

We have already seen in the previous chapter how you can get help using MATLAB's drop down menus.

But, in addition, support can also be obtained via commands (instructions or functions), implemented as MATLAB objects.

You can use the help command to get immediate access to diverse information.

```
» help

HELP topics:

matlab\general     -  General purpose commands.
matlab\ops         -  Operators and special characters.
matlab\lang        -  Programming language constructs.
matlab\elmat       -  Elementary matrices and matrix manipulation.
matlab\elfun       -  Elementary math functions.
matlab\specfun     -  Specialized math functions.
matlab\matfun      -  Matrix functions - numerical linear algebra.
matlab\datafun     -  Data analysis and Fourier transforms.
matlab\polyfun     -  Interpolation and polynomials.
matlab\funfun      -  Function functions and ODE solvers.
matlab\sparfun     -  Sparse matrices.
matlab\graph2d     -  Two dimensional graphs.
matlab\graph3d     -  Three dimensional graphs.
matlab\specgraph   -  Specialized graphs.
matlab\graphics    -  Handle Graphics.
matlab\uitools     -  Graphical user interface tools.
matlab\strfun      -  Character strings.
matlab\iofun       -  File input/output.
matlab\timefun     -  Time and dates.
matlab\datatypes   -  Data types and structures.
matlab\winfun      -  Windows Operating System Interface Files(DDE/ActiveX)
matlab\demos       -  Examples and demonstrations.
toolbox\symbolic   -  Symbolic Math Toolbox.
toolbox\tour       -  MATLAB Tour
toolbox\local      -  Preferences.

For more help on directory/topic, type "help topic".
```

As we can see, the help command displays a list of program directories and their contents. Help on any given topic *topic* can be displayed using the command *help topic*. For example:

```
» help inv

INV    Matrix inverse.
INV(X) is the inverse of the square matrix X.
A warning message is printed if X is badly scaled or
nearly singular.
```

See also SLASH, PINV, COND, CONDEST, NNLS, LSCOV.

Overloaded methods
help sym/inv.m

» help matlab\elfun

Elementary math functions.

Trigonometric.

sin	*- Sine.*
sinh	*- Hyperbolic sine.*
asin	*- Inverse sine.*
asinh	*- Inverse hyperbolic sine.*
cos	*- Cosine.*
cosh	*- Hyperbolic cosine.*
acos	*- Inverse cosine.*
acosh	*- Inverse hyperbolic cosine.*
tan	*- Tangent.*
tanh	*- Hyperbolic tangent.*
atan	*- Inverse tangent.*
atan2	*- Four quadrant inverse tangent.*
atanh	*- Inverse hyperbolic tangent.*
sec	*- Secant.*
sech	*- Hyperbolic secant.*
asec	*- Inverse secant.*
asech	*- Inverse hyperbolic secant.*
csc	*- Cosecant.*
csch	*- Hyperbolic cosecant.*
acsc	*- Inverse cosecant.*
acsch	*- Inverse hyperbolic cosecant.*
cot	*- Cotangent.*
coth	*- Hyperbolic cotangent.*
acot	*- Inverse cotangent.*
acoth	*- Inverse hyperbolic cotangent.*

Exponential.

exp	*- Exponential.*
log	*- Natural logarithm.*
log10	*- Common(base 10) logarithm.*
log2	*- Base 2 logarithm and dissect floating point number.*
pow2	*- Base 2 power and scale floating point number.*
sqrt	*- Square root.*
nextpow2	*- Next higher power of 2.*

Complex.

```
abs        - Absolute value.
angle      - Phase angle.
conj       - Complex conjugate.
imag       - Complex imaginary part.
real       - Complex real part.
unwrap     - Unwrap phase angle.
isreal     - True for real array.
cplxpair   - Sort numbers into complex conjugate pairs.
```

Rounding and remainder.

```
fix        - Round towards zero.
floor      - Round towards minus infinity.
ceil       - Round towards plus infinity.
round      - Round towards nearest integer.
mod        - Modulus(signed remainder after division).
rem        - Remainder after division.
sign       - Signum.
```

There is a command for help on a certain sequence of characters (*lookfor string*) which allows you to find all those functions or commands that contain or refer to the given string *string*. This command is very useful when there is no direct support for the specified string, or if you want to view the help for all commands related to the given sequence. For example, if we seek help for all commands that contain the sequence *complex*, we can use the *lookfor complex* command to see which commands MATLAB provides.

» lookfor complex

```
ctranspose.m: %'   Complex conjugate transpose.
CONJ    Complex conjugate.
CPLXPAIR Sort numbers into complex conjugate pairs.
IMAG    Complex imaginary part.
REAL    Complex real part.
CDF2RDF Complex diagonal form to real block diagonal form.
RSF2CSF Real block diagonal form to complex diagonal form.
B5ODE   Stiff problem, linear with complex eigenvalues(B5 of EHL).
CPLXDEMO Maps of functions of a complex variable.
CPLXGRID Polar coordinate complex grid.
CPLXMAP Plot a function of a complex variable.
GRAFCPLX Demonstrates complex function plots in MATLAB.
ctranspose.m: %TRANSPOSE Symbolic matrix complex conjugate transpose.
SMOKE   Complex matrix with a "smoke ring" pseudospectrum.
```

MATLAB and Programming

By properly combining all the objects defined in MATLAB, according to the rules of syntax of the program, you can build useful mathematical research programming code. Programs usually consist of a series of instructions in which values are calculated, are assigned names and are reused in further calculations.

As in programming languages like C or FORTRAN, in MATLAB you can write programs with loops, control flow and conditionals. MATLAB can write procedural programs, i.e., it can define a sequence of standard steps to run. As in C or Pascal, a Do, For, or While loop can be used for repetitive calculations. The language of MATLAB also includes conditional constructs such as If—Then—Else. MATLAB also supports different logical operators, such as AND, OR, NOT and XOR.

MATLAB supports procedural programming (with iterative processes, recursive functions, loops, etc.), functional programming and object-oriented programming. Here are two simple examples of programs. The first generates the Hilbert matrix of order n, and the second calculates all the Fibonacci numbers less than 1000.

```
% Generating the Hilbert matrix of order n
t = '1/(i+j-1)';
for i = 1:n
for j = 1:n
a(i,j) = eval(t);
end
end

% Calculating the Fibonacci numbers
f = [1 1]; i = 1;
while f(i) + f(i-1) < 1000
f(i+2) = f(i) + f(i+1);
i = i+1
end
```

Commands to Escape and Exit to the MS-DOS Environment

There are three ways you can escape from the MATLAB Command Window to the MS-DOS operating system environment in order to run temporary assignments. Entering the command ! *dos_command* in the Command Window allows you to run the specified DOS command in the MATLAB environment. For example:

```
! dir
```

```
The volume of drive D has no label
The volume serial number £ is 145 c-12F2
Directory of D:\MATLAB52\bin

.                <DIR>        13/03/98   0:16 .
..               <DIR>        13/03/98   0:16 ..
BCCOPTS  BAT        1.872     19/01/98  14:14 bccopts.bat
CLBS110  DLL      219.136     21/08/97  22:24 clbs110.dll
CMEX     BAT        2.274     13/03/98   0:28 cmex.bat
COMPTOOL BAT       34.992     19/01/98  14:14 comptool.bat
DF500PTS BAT        1.973     19/01/98  14:14 df50opts.bat
FENG     DLL       25.088     18/12/97  16:34 feng.dll
FMAT     DLL       16.896     18/12/97  16:34 fmat.dll
FMEX     BAT        2.274     13/03/98   0:28 fmex.bat
LICENSE  DAT          470     13/03/98   0:27 license.dat
W32SSI   DLL       66.560     02/05/97   8:34 w32ssi.dll
10 file(s)        11.348.865 bytes
directory(s) 159.383.552 bytes free
```

The command ! *dos_command* & is used to execute the specified DOS command in background mode. The command is executed by opening a DOS environment window on the MATLAB Command Window, as shown in Figure 1-29. To return to the MATLAB environment simply right-click anywhere in the Command Window (the DOS environment window will close automatically). You can return to the DOS window at any time to run any operating system command by clicking the icon labeled *MS-DOS symbol* at the bottom of the screen.

Figure 1-29.

The command >>*dos_command* is used to execute the DOS command in the MATLAB screen. Using the three previous commands, not only DOS commands, but also all kinds of executable files or batch tasks can be executed (Figure 1-30).

```
>> dir

.               ..              fixedponit.m  g1.asv      g1.m

>> type g1.m

function g=g1(x)
g=x^2-sin(x+0.15);

fx >> |
```

Figure 1-30.

The command >>*dos dos_command* is also used to execute the specified DOS command in automatic mode in the MATLAB Command Window (Figure 1-31).

```
>> dos dir

16/06/2014   17:26    <DIR>           .
16/06/2014   17:26    <DIR>           ..
16/06/2014   17:03                420 fixedponit.m
17/06/2014   16:48                 92 g1.asv
16/06/2014   17:28                 38 g1.m
```

Figure 1-31.

To exit MATLAB, simply type *quit* in the Command Window, and then press *Enter*.

■ ■ ■

CHAPTER 2

First Order Differential Equations. Exact Equations, Separation of Variables, Homogeneous and Linear Equations

First Order Differential Equations

Although it implements only a relatively small number of commands related to this topic, MATLAB's treatment of differential equations is nevertheless very efficient. We shall see how we can use these commands to solve each type of differential equation algebraically. Numerical methods for the approximate solution of equations and systems of equations are also implemented.

The basic command used to solve differential equations is **dsolve**. This command finds symbolic solutions of ordinary differential equations and systems of ordinary differential equations. The equations are specified by symbolic expressions where the letter D is used to denote differentiation, or D2, D3, etc, to denote differentiation of order 2,3,..., etc. The letter preceded by D (or D2, etc) is the dependent variable (which is usually y), and any letter that is not preceded by D (or D2, etc) is a candidate for the independent variable. If the independent variable is not specified, it is taken to be x by default. If x is specified as the dependent variable, then the independent variable is t. That is, x is the independent variable by default, unless it is declared as the dependent variable, in which case the independent variable is understood to be t.

You can specify initial conditions using additional equations, which take the form $y(a) = b$ or $Dy(a) = b$,..., etc. If the initial conditions are not specified, the solutions of the differential equations will contain constants of integration, C1, C2,..., etc. The most important MATLAB commands that solve differential equations are the following:

dsolve('equation', 'v'): **This solves the given differential equation, where v is the independent variable (if 'v' is not specified, the independent variable is x by default). This returns only explicit solutions.**

dsolve('equation', 'initial_condition',..., 'v'): **This solves the given differential equation subject to the specified initial condition.**

dsolve('equation', 'cond1', 'cond2',..., 'condn', 'v'): **This solves the given differential equation subject to the specified initial conditions.**

dsolve('equation', 'cond1, cond2,..., condn', 'v'): **This solves the given differential equation subject to the specified initial conditions.**

dsolve('eq1', 'eq2',..., 'eqn', 'cond1', 'cond2',..., 'condn' , 'v'): **This solves the given system of differential equations subject to the specified initial conditions.**

dsolve('eq1, eq2,..., eqn', 'cond1, cond2,..., condn' , 'v'): This solves the given system of differential equations subject to the specified initial conditions.

maple('dsolve(equation, func(var))'): This solves the given differential equation, where var is the independent variable and func is the dependent variable (returns implicit solutions).

maple('dsolve({equation, cond1, cond2,... condn}, func(var))'): This solves the given differential equation subject to the specified initial conditions.

maple('dsolve({eq1, eq2,..., eqn}, {func1(var), func2(var),... funcn(var)})'): This solves the given system of differential equations (returns implicit solutions).

maple('dsolve(equation, func(var), 'explicit')'): This solves the given differential equation, offering the solution in explicit form, if possible.

Examples are given below.

First, we solve differential equations of first order and first degree, both with and without initial values.

» **pretty(dsolve('Dy = a*y'))**

```
 C2 exp(a t)
```

» **pretty(dsolve('Df = f + sin(t)'))**

```
             sin(t)   cos(t)
 C6 exp(t) - ------ - ------
               2        2
```

The previous two equations can also be solved in the following way:

» **pretty(sym(maple('dsolve(diff(y(x), x) = a * y, y(x))')))**

```
y(x) = exp(a x) _C1
```

» **pretty(maple('dsolve(diff(f(t),t)=f+sin(t),f(t))'))**

```
f(t) = - 1/2 cos(t) - 1/2 sin(t) + exp(t) _C1
```

» **pretty(dsolve('Dy = a*y', 'y(0) = b'))**

```
exp(a x) b
```

» **pretty(dsolve('Df = f + sin(t)', 'f(pi/2) = 0'))**

```
    /   pi \
  exp| - -- | exp(t)
    \   2  /              sin(t)   cos(t)
  ------------------- - ------ - ------
          2               2        2
```

Now we solve an equation of second degree and first order.

» **y = dsolve('(Dy) ^ 2 + y ^ 2 = 1', ' y(0) = 0', 's')**

```
y =

 cosh((pi*i)/2 + s*i)
 cosh((pi*i)/2 - s*i)
```

We can also solve this in the following way:

» pretty(maple('dsolve({diff(y(s),s)^2 + y(s)^2 = 1, y(0) = 0}, y(s))'))

$y(s) = sin(s)$, $y(s) = - sin(s)$

Now we solve an equation of second order and first degree.

» pretty(dsolve('D2y = - a ^ 2 * y ', 'y(0) = 1, Dy(pi/a) = 0'))

```
exp(-a t i)    exp(a t i)
----------- + ----------
     2             2
```

Next we solve a couple of systems, both with and without initial values.

»> dsolve('Dx = y', 'Dy = -x')

ans =

```
    y: [1x1 sym]
    x: [1x1 sym]
```

»> y

y =

```
 cosh((pi*i)/2 + s*i)
 cosh((pi*i)/2 - s*i)
```

»> x

x =

x

»> y=dsolve('Df = 3*f+4*g', 'Dg = -4*f+3*g')

y =

```
    g: [1x1 sym]
    f: [1x1 sym]
```

»> y.g

ans =

$C27*cos(4*t)*exp(3*t) - C28*sin(4*t)*exp(3*t)$

```
>> y.f
```

ans =

C28*cos(4*t)*exp(3*t) + C27*sin(4*t)*exp(3*t)

```
>> y=dsolve('Df = 3*f+4*g, Dg = -4*f+3*g', 'f(0)=0, g(0)=1')
```

y =

   g: [1x1 sym]
   f: [1x1 sym]

```
>> y.g
```

ans =

cos(4*t)*exp(3*t)

```
>> y.f
```

ans =

sin(4*t)*exp(3*t)

This last system can also be solved in the following way:

```
» pretty(maple('dsolve({diff(f(x),x)= 3*f(x)+4*g(x), diff(g(x),x)=-4*f(x)+3*g(x),
f(0)=0,g(0)=1}, {f(x),g(x)})'))
```

{f(x) = exp(3 x) sin(4 x), g(x) = exp(3 x) cos(4 x)}

Separation of Variables

A differential equation is said to have separable variables if it can be written in the form

$$f(x)dx=g(y)dy.$$

This type of equation can be solved immediately by putting $\int f(x)dx=\int g(y)dy+c.$

If MATLAB cannot directly solve a differential equation with the function *dsolve*, then we can try to express it in the above form and solve the given integrals algebraically, which does not present particular difficulties for the program, given its versatility in symbolic computation.

EXERCISE 2-1

Solve the differential equation:

$$y\cos(x)\,dx-(1+y^2)\,dy=0, y(0)=1.$$

First of all we try to solve it directly. The equation can be written in the form:

$$y'(x)=\frac{\cos(x)y(x)}{1+y(x)^2}.$$

```
» dsolve('Dy = y * cos(x) /(1+y^2)')
```

ans =

*exp(C33 + t*cos(x))*exp(-wrightOmega(2*C33 + 2*t*cos(x))/2)*⁰

Thus the differential equation appears not to be solvable with *dsolve*. However, in this case, the variables are separable, so we can solve the equation as follows:

```
» pretty(solve('int(cos(x), x) = int((1+y^2) / y, y)'))
```

```
+-                        -+
|          /        2 \    |
|          |       y  |    |
|    asin| log(y) + -- |    |
|          \       2  /    |
|                          |
|          /        2 \  | |
|          |       y  |  | |
|  pi - asin| log(y) + -- |  | |
|          \       2  /  | |
+-                        -+
```

Thus, after a little rearrangement, we see that the general solution is given by:

$$\sin(x)=\log(y)+1/2\,y^2+C.$$

We now find the value of the constant *C* via the initial condition, putting $x=0$ and $y=1$.

```
» C = simple('solve(subs(x = 0, y = 1, sin(x) = log(y) + 1/2 * y ^ 2 + C), C)')
```

C =

-1/2

Thus the final solution is $\sin(x)=\log(y)+1/2\,y^2-½$.

In the same way you can solve any other differential equation with separable variables.

The above differential equation is also solvable directly by using:

```
» pretty(maple('dsolve(diff(y(x), x) = y(x) * cos(x) /(1 + y(x) ^ 2), y(x))'))
```

$$\log(y(x)) + 1/2\ y(x)^2 - \sin(x) = \_C1$$

Homogeneous Differential Equations

Consider a general differential equation of first degree and first order of the form

$$M(x,y)dx = N(x,y)dy.$$

This equation is said to be homogeneous of degree n if the functions M and N satisfy:

$$M(tx,ty) = t^n M(x,y),$$
$$N(tx,ty) = t^n N(x,y),$$

For this type of equation, we can transform the initial differential equation (with variables x and y), via the change of variable $x = vy$, into another (separable) equation (with variables v and y). The new equation is solved by separation of variables and then the solution of the original equation is found by reversing the change of variable.

EXERCISE 2-2

Solve the differential equation:

$$(x^2 - y^2)dx + x\,y\,dy = 0.$$

First we check if the equation is homogeneous

```
» maple('m:=(x,y) - > x ^ 2 - y ^ 2');
» maple('n:=(x,y) - > x * y ');
» factor('m(t*x,t*y)')
```

ans =

$t \wedge 2\ *(x{-}y)\ *(x + y)$

```
» factor('n(t*x,t*y)')
```

ans =

$t \wedge 2 * x * y$

Thus the equation is homogeneous of degree 2. To solve it we apply the change of variable $x = vy$.

Before performing the change of variable, it is advisable to load the library *difforms*, using the command **maple('with(difforms)')**, which will allow you to work with differential forms. Once this library is loaded it is also convenient to use the command **maple('defform(v=0,x=0,y=0)')**, which allows you to declare all variables which will not be constants or parameters in the differentiation.

```
» maple('with(difforms)');
» maple('defform(v=0,x=0,y=0)');
```

Now we can make the change of variable $x = vy$, and group the terms in d(v) and d(y).

```
» simplify('subs(x = v * y m(x,y) * d(x) + n(x,y) * d(y))')
```

ans =

```
v ^ 2 * y ^ 3 * d(v) + v ^ 3 * y ^ 2 * d(y) - y ^ 3 * d(v)
```

```
» pretty(maple('collect(v ^ 2 * y ^ 3 * d(v) + v ^ 3 * y ^ 2 * d(y) - y ^ 3 * d(v)
{d(v), d(y)})'))
```

$$(v^2 y^2 - y^2)(y\, d(v) + v\, d(y)) + y^2 v\, d(y)$$

If we divide the previous expression by $v^3 y^3$, and group the terms in d(v) and d(y), we already have an equation in separated variables.

```
» pretty(maple('collect((((v^2*y^3-y^3) * d(v) + v ^ 3 * y ^ 2 * d(y)) /(v^3*y^3),
{d(v), d(y)})'))
```

$$\frac{(v^2 y^3 - y^3)\, d(v)}{v^3 y^3} + \frac{d(y)}{y}$$

The previous expression can be simplified.

```
» pretty(maple('convert(collect((((v^2*y^3-y^3) * d(v) + v ^ 3 * y ^ 2 * d(y))
/(v^3*y^3), {d(v), d(y)}), parfrac, y)'))
```

$$\frac{(v^2 - 1)\, d(v)}{v^3} + \frac{d(y)}{y}$$

Now, we solve the equation:

```
» pretty(simple('int((v^2-1)/v ^ 3, v) + int(1/y,y)'))
```

$$log(v) + \frac{1}{2\ v^2} + log(y)$$

Finally we reverse the change of variable:

```
» pretty(simple('subs(v = x / y log(v) + 1/2/v ^ 2 + log(y))'))
```

$$log(x) + \frac{1}{2}\ \frac{y^2}{x^2}$$

Thus the general solution of the original differential equation is:

$$\log(x)+\frac{1}{2}\frac{y^2}{x^2}=C.$$

Now we can represent the solutions of this differential equation graphically. To do this we graph the solutions with parameter C, which is equivalent to the following contour plot of the function defined by the left-hand side of the above general solution (see Figure 18-1):

```
» [x,y]=meshgrid(0.1:0.05:1/2,-1:0.05:1);
» z=y.^2./(2*x.^2)+log(x);
» contour(z,65)
```

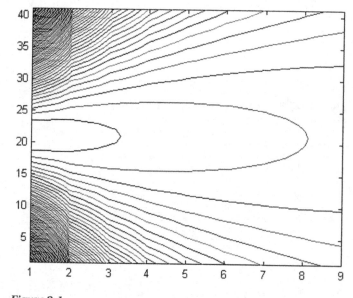

Figure 2-1.

Exact Differential Equations

The differential equation

$$M(x,y)dx + N(x,y)dy = 0$$

is said to be exact if $\partial N/\partial x = \partial M/\partial y$. If the equation is exact, then there exists a function F such that its total differential dF coincides with the left-hand side of the above equation, i.e.:

$$dF = M(x,y)dx + N(x,y)dy$$

therefore the family of solutions is given by $F(x,y) = C$.

The exercise below follows the usual steps of an algebraic solution to this type of equation.

EXERCISE 2-3

Solve the differential equation:

$$\left(-1 + ye^{xy} + y\cos(xy)\right)dx + \left(1 + xe^{xy} + x\cos(xy)\right)dy = 0$$

First of all, we try to solve the equation with *dsolve*:

```
» maple('m:=(x,y) - > - 1 + y * exp(x*y) + y * cos(x*y)');
» maple('n:=(x,y) - > 1 + x * exp(x*y) + x * cos(x*y)');
» dsolve('m(x,y) + n(x,y) * Dy = 0')
```

```
??? Error using ==> dsolve
Explicit solution could not be found.
```

Thus the function *dsolve* does not give a solution to the proposed equation. We are going to try to solve the equation using the classical algebraic method.

First we check that the proposed differential equation is exact.

```
» pretty(simple(diff('m(x,y)','y')))
```

```
exp(y x) + x y exp(y x) + cos(y x) - x sin(y x) y
```

```
» pretty(simple(diff('n(x,y)','x')))
```

```
exp(y x) + x y exp(y x) + cos(y x) - x sin(y x) y
```

Since the equation is exact, we can find the solution in the following way:

```
» solution1 = simplify('int(m(x,y), x) + g(y)')
```

```
solution1 =
```

```
-x+exp(y*x) + sin(y*x) + g(y)
```

41

Now we find the function $g(y)$ via the following condition:

$$\text{diff}\left(\text{int}(m(x,y),x)+g(y),y\right)=n(x,y)$$

» **pretty(simplify('int(m(x,y), x) + g(y)'))**

$$-x + exp(y\ x) + sin(y\ x) + g(y)$$

» **pretty(simplify('diff(-x+exp(y*x) + sin(y*x) + g(y), y)'))**

$$x\ exp(y\ x)\ x + x\ cos(y\ x) + \frac{d}{dy}\ g(y)$$

» **simplify('solve(x * exp(y*x) + x * cos(y*x) + diff(g(y), y) = n(x,y), diff(g(y), y))')**

ans =

1

Thus $g'(y) = 1$, so the final solution will be, omitting the addition of a constant:

» **pretty(simplify('subs(g(y) = int(1,y),-x+exp(y*x) + sin(y*x) + g(y))'))**

$$-x + exp(y\ x) + sin(y\ x) + y$$

To graphically represent the family of solutions, we draw the following contour plot of the above expression (Figure 18-2):

```
» [x,y]=meshgrid(-2*pi/3:.2:2*pi/3);
» z =-x+exp(y.*x) + sin(y.*x) + y;
» contour(z,100)
```

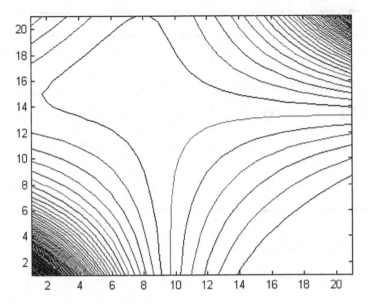

Figure 2-2.

In the following section we will see how any reducible differential equation can be transformed to an exact equation using an **integrating factor**.

Linear Differential Equations

A linear first order differential equation is an equation of the form:

$$dy/dx + P(x)y = Q(x)$$

where $P(x)$ and $Q(x)$ are given functions of x.

Differential equations of this type can be transformed into exact equations by multiplying both sides of the equation by the integrating factor:

$$e^{\int P(x)dx}$$

and the general solution is then given by the expression:

$$\left(e^{-\int P(x)dx}\right)\left(\int e^{\int P(x)dx}Q(x)dx\right)$$

MATLAB implements these solutions of linear differential equations, and offers them whenever the integral appearing in the integrating factor can be found.

EXERCISE 2-4

Solve the differential equation:

$$x\,dy/dx + 3\,y = x\sin(x).$$

```
» pretty(simple(dsolve('x * Dy + 3 * y = x * sin(x)')))
```

```
                     /   3 t \
               C36 exp| - --- |
    x sin(x)          \   x  /
    -------- - ----------------
       3              3
```

CHAPTER 3

■ ■ ■

Higher Order Differential Equations. The Laplace Transform and Special Types of Equations

Ordinary High-Order Equations

An **ordinary linear differential equation of order n** has the following general form:

$$\sum_{k=0}^{n} a_k(x)y^{(k)}(x) = a_0(x)y(x) + a_1(x)y'(x) + a_2(x)y''(x) + \ldots + a_n(x)y^{(n)}(x)$$

$$= f(x).$$

If the function $f(x)$ is identically zero, the equation is called **homogeneous**. Otherwise, the equation is called **non-homogeneous**. If the functions $a_i(x)$ $(i = 1, \ldots, n)$ are constant, the equation is said to have **constant coefficients**.

A concept of great importance in this context is that of a set of **linearly independent functions**. A set of functions $\{f_1(x), f_2(x), \ldots, f_n(x)\}$ is linearly independent if, for any x in their common domain of definition, the Wronskian determinant of the functions is non-zero. The **Wronskian determinant** of the given set of functions, at a point x of their common domain of definition, is defined as follows:

$$\begin{vmatrix} f_1(x) & f_2(x) & f_3(x) & \cdots & f_n(x) \\ f_1'(x) & f_2'(x) & f_3'(x) & \cdots & f_n'(x) \\ f_1''(x) & f_2''(x) & f_3''(x) & \cdots & f_n''(x) \\ \cdots & \cdots & \cdots & \cdots & \cdots \\ f_1^{(n-1)}(x) & f_2^{(n-1)}(x) & f_3^{(n-1)}(x) & \cdots & f_n^{(n-1)}(x) \end{vmatrix} = W(x).$$

The MATLAB command *maple('Wronskian')* allows you to calculate the Wronskian matrix of a set of functions. Its syntax is:

maple('Wronskian(V,x)'): This computes the Wronskian matrix corresponding to the vector of functions V with independent variable x.

A set $S = \{f_1(x), \ldots, f_n(x)\}$ of linearly independent non-trivial solutions of a homogeneous linear equation of order n

$$a_0(x)y(x) + a_1(x)y'(x) + a_2(x)y''(x) + \cdots + a_n(x)y^{(n)}(x) = 0$$

is called a set of **fundamental solutions of the equation**.

If the functions $a_i(x)$ $(i=1,...,n)$ are continuous in an open interval I, then the homogeneous equation has a set of fundamental solutions $S = \{f_i(x)\}$ in I.

In addition, the general solution of the homogeneous equation will then be given by the function:

$$f(x) = \sum_{i=0}^{n} c_i f_i(x)$$

where $\{c_i\}$ is a set of arbitrary constants.

The equation:

$$a_0 + a_1 m + a_2 m^2 + \cdots + a_n m^n = \sum_{i=0}^{n} a_i m^i = 0$$

is called the **characteristic equation** of the homogeneous differential equation with constant coefficients. The solutions of this characteristic equation determine the general solutions of the corresponding differential equation.

EXERCISE 3-1

Show that the set of functions

$$\{e^x, xe^x, x^2 e^x\}$$

is linearly independent.

» **indfunctions = maple('vector([exp(x), x * exp(x), x ^ 2 * exp(x)])')**

indfunctions =

*[exp(x), x * exp(x), x ^ 2 * exp(x)]*

» **W=maple('Wronskian(indfunctions,x)')**

W =

[exp(x),   x*exp(x),   x^2*exp(x)]
[exp(x),   exp(x)+x*exp(x),   2*x*exp(x)+x^2*exp(x)]
[exp(x), 2*exp(x)+x*exp(x), 2*exp(x)+4*x*exp(x)+x^2*exp(x)]

» **pretty(determ(W))**

```
        3
2 exp(x)
```

This gives us the value of the Wronskian, which is obviously always non-zero. Therefore the set of functions is linearly independent.

Linear Higher-Order Equations. Homogeneous Equations with Constant Coefficients

The homogeneous linear differential equation of order n

$$\sum_{k=0}^{n} a_k(x) y^{(k)}(x) = a_0(x)y(x) + a_1(x)y'(x) + a_2(x)y''(x) + \cdots + a_n(x)y^{(n)}(x)$$
$$= 0$$

is said to have **constant coefficients** if the functions $a_i(x)$ $(i = 1, ..., n)$ are all constant (i.e. they do not depend on the variable x).

The equation:

$$a_0 + a_1 m + a_2 m^2 + \cdots + a_n m^n = \sum_{i=0}^{n} a_i m^i = 0$$

is called the **characteristic equation** of the above differential equation. The solutions $(m_1, m_2, ..., m_n)$ of this characteristic equation determine the general solution of the associated differential equation.

If the mi $(i = 1, ..., n)$ are all different, the general solution of the homogeneous equation with constant coefficients is:

$$y(x) = c_1 e^{m_1 x} + c_2 e^{m_2 x} + \cdots + c_n e^{m_n x}$$

where $c_1, c_2, ..., c_n$ are arbitrary constants.

If some m_i is a root of multiplicity k of the characteristic equation, then it determines the following k terms of the solution:

$$c_i e^{m_i x} + c_{i+1} x e^{m_i x} + c_{i+2} x^2 e^{m_i x} + \cdots + c_{i+k} x^k e^{m_i x}.$$

If the characteristic equation has a complex root $m_j = a + bi$, then its complex conjugate $m_{j+1} = a - bi$ is also a root. These two roots determine a pair of terms in the general solution of the homogeneous equation:

$$c_j e^{ax} \cos(bx) + c_{j+1} e^{ax} \sin(bx).$$

MATLAB directly applies this method to obtain the solutions of homogeneous linear equations with constant coefficients, using the command *dsolve* or *maple('dsolve')*.

EXERCISE 3-2

Solve the following equations:

$$3y'' + 2y' - 5y = 0$$

$$2y'' + 5y' + 5y = 0, \quad y(0) = 0, \quad y'(0) = \tfrac{1}{2}.$$

```
» pretty(dsolve('3*D2y+2*Dy-5*y=0'))

                  /   5 t \
    C38 exp(t) + C39 exp| - --- |
                  \   3 /
```

» **pretty(dsolve('2 * D2y + 5 * Dy + 5 * y = 0', ' y(0) = 0 Dy(0) = 1/2 '))**

```
                          /    1/2   \
        1/2    /   5 t \   | 15      t |
     2 15     exp| - --- | sin| ------- |
                  \   4 /   \    4    /
     ----------------------------------
                      15
```

EXERCISE 3-3

Solve the differential equation

$$9y'''' - 6y''' + 46y'' - 6y' + 37y = 0.$$

» **pretty(simple(dsolve('9*D4y-6*D3y+46*D2y-6*Dy+37*y=0')))**

```
                                    / t \                      / t \
C46 cos(t) + C47 sin(t) + C44 cos(2 t) exp| - | + C45 sin(2 t) exp| - |
                                    \ 3 /                      \ 3 /
```

Looking at the solution, it is evident that the characteristic equation has two pairs of complex conjugate solutions.

» **solve('9*x^4-6*x^3+46*x^2-6*x+37=0')**

ans =

```
          i
         -i
   1/3 + 2*i
   1/3 - 2*i
```

Non-Homogeneous Equations with Constant Coefficients. Variation of Parameters

Consider the non-homogeneous linear equation with constant coefficients:

$$\sum_{k=0}^{n} a_k(x)y^{(k)}(x) = a_0(x)y(x) + a_1(x)y'(x) + a_2(x)y''(x) + \cdots + a_n(x)y^{(n)}(x)$$

$$= f(x).$$

Suppose $\{y_1(x), y_2(x),\ldots, y_n(x)\}$ is a linearly independent set of solutions of the corresponding homogeneous equation:

$$a_0(x)y(x) + a_1(x)y'(x) + a_2(x)y''(x) + \cdots + a_n(x)y^{(n)}(x) = 0.$$

A **particular solution of the non-homogeneous equation** is given by:

$$y_p(x) = \sum_{i=1}^{n} u_i(x) y_i(x)$$

where the functions $u_i(x)$ are obtained as follows:

$$u_i(x) = \int \frac{f(x) W_i[y_1(x), y_2(x), ..., y_n(x)]}{W[y_1(x), y_2(x), ..., y_n(x)]} dx \quad (i = 1, ..., n).$$

Here $W_i[y_1(x), y_2(x), ..., y_n(x)]$ is the determinant of the matrix obtained by replacing the i-th column of the Wronskian matrix $W[y_1(x), y_2(x), ..., y_n(x)]$ by the transpose of the vector $(0, 0, ..., 0, 1)$.

The solution of the non-homogeneous equation is then given by combining the general solution of the homogeneous equation with the particular solution of the non-homogeneous equation. If the roots m_i of the characteristic equation of the homogeneous equation are all different, the general solution of the non-homogeneous equation is:

$$y(x) = c_1 e^{m_1 x} + c_2 e^{m_2 x} + ... + c_n e^{m_n x} + y_p(x).$$

If some of the roots are repeated, we refer to the general form of the solution of a homogeneous equation discussed earlier.

EXERCISE 3-4

Solve the following differential equations:

$$y'' + 4y' + 13y = x\cos^2(3x),$$

$$y'' - 2y' + y = e^x \ln(x).$$

We will follow the algebraic method of variation of parameters to solve the first equation. We first consider the characteristic equation of the homogeneous equation to obtain a set of linearly independent solutions.

```
» solve('m^2+4*m+13=0')

ans =

[- 2 + 3 * i]
[- 2 - 3 * i]

» maple('f: = x - > x * cos(3*x) ^ 2');
» maple('y1: = x - > exp(-2*x) * cos(3*x)');
» maple('y2: = x - > exp(-2*x) * sin(3*x)');
» maple('W: = x - > Wronskian([y1(x), y2(x)], x)');
» pretty(simplify(maple('det(W(x))')))

3 exp(-4 x)
```

We see that the Wronskian is non-zero, indicating that the functions are linearly independent. Now we calculate the functions $W_i(x)$, $i=1,2$.

```
» maple('W1: x-= > array([[0, y2(x)], [1, diff((y2)(x), x)]])');
» pretty(simplify(maple('det(W1(x))')))
```

$-exp(-2\ x)\ sin(3\ x)$

```
» maple('W2: x-= > array([[y1(x), 0], [diff((y1)(x), x), 1]])');
» pretty(simplify(maple('det(W2(x))')))
```

$exp(-2\ x)\ cos(3\ x)$

Now we calculate the particular solution of the non-homogeneous equation.

```
» maple('u1:=x->factor(simplify(int(f(x)*det(W1(x))/det(W(x)),x)))');
» maple('u1(x)')
```

ans =

$1/14652300*exp(2*x)*(129285*cos(9*x)*x-6084*cos(9*x)-28730*sin(9*x)*x-$
$13013*sin(9*x)+281775*cos(3*x)*x-86700*cos(3*x)-187850*sin(3*x)*x-36125*sin(3*x))$

```
» maple('u2:=x->factor(simplify(int(f(x)*det(W2(x))/det(W(x)),x)))');
» maple('u2(x)')
```

ans =

$1/14652300 * exp(2*x) *(563550 * cos(3*x) * x+108375 * cos(3*x) + 845325 * sin(3*x) * x-260100$
$* sin(3*x) + 28730 * cos(9*x) * x+13013 * cos(9*x) + 129285 * sin(9*x) * x-6084 * sin(9*x))$

```
» maple('yp: = x - > factor(simplify(y1(x) *(x) u1 + y2(x) * u2(x)))');
» maple('yp(x)')
```

ans =

$-23/1105 * x * cos(3*x) \wedge 2 + 13436/1221025 * cos(3*x) \wedge 2 + 24/1105 * cos(3*x) * sin(3*x)$
$* x + 3852/1221025 * cos(3*x) * sin(3*x) + 54/1105 * x-21168/1221025$

Then we can write the general solution of the non-homogeneous equation:

```
» maple(' y: = x - > simplify(c1 * y1(x) + c2 * y2(x) + yp(x))');
» maple('combine(and(x), trig)')
```

ans =

$C1 * exp(-2*x) * cos(3*x) + c2 * exp(-2*x) * sin(3*x)-23/2210 * x * cos(6*x) + 1/26$
$* x + 6718/1221025 * cos(6*x)-2/169 + 12/1105 * x * sin(6*x) + 1926/1221025 * sin(6*x)$

Now we graphically represent a set of solutions, for certain values of c1 and c2 (see Figure 3-1)

```
» fplot(simplify('subs(c1=-5,c2=-4,y(x))'),[-1,1])
» hold on
» fplot(simplify('subs(c1=-5,c2=4,y(x))'),[-1,1])
» fplot(simplify('subs(c1=-5,c2=2,y(x))'),[-1,1])
» fplot(simplify('subs(c1=-5,c2=-2,y(x))'),[-1,1])
» fplot(simplify('subs(c1=-5,c2=-1,y(x))'),[-1,1])
» fplot(simplify('subs(c1=-5,c2=1,y(x))'),[-1,1])
» fplot(simplify('subs(c1=5,c2=1,y(x))'),[-1,1])
» fplot(simplify('subs(c1=5,c2=-1,y(x))'),[-1,1])
» fplot(simplify('subs(c1=5,c2=-2,y(x))'),[-1,1])
» fplot(simplify('subs(c1=5,c2=2,y(x))'),[-1,1])
» fplot(simplify('subs(c1=5,c2=4,y(x))'),[-1,1])
» fplot(simplify('subs(c1=5,c2=-4,y(x))'),[-1,1])
» fplot(simplify('subs(c1=0,c2=-4,y(x))'),[-1,1])
» fplot(simplify('subs(c1=0,c2=4,y(x))'),[-1,1])
» fplot(simplify('subs(c1=0,c2=2,y(x))'),[-1,1])
» fplot(simplify('subs(c1=0,c2=-2,y(x))'),[-1,1])
» fplot(simplify('subs(c1=0,c2=-1,y(x))'),[-1,1])
» fplot(simplify('subs(c1=0,c2=1,y(x))'),[-1,1])
```

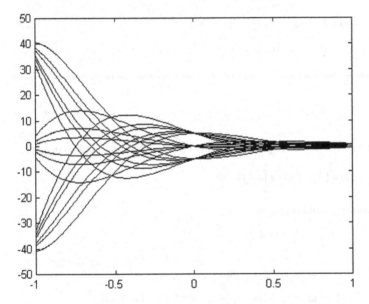

Figure 3-1.

For the second differential equation we directly apply *dsolve*, obtaining the solution:

```
» pretty(simple(dsolve('D2y-2 * Dy + y = exp(x) * log(x)')))
```

exp(x) log(x) + C49 exp(t) + C50 t exp(t)

Non-Homogeneous Equations with Variable Coefficients. Cauchy–Euler Equations

A non-homogeneous linear equation with variable coefficients of the form

$$\sum_{k=0}^{n} a_k x^k y^{(k)}(x) = a_0 y(x) + a_1 xy'(x) + a_2 x^2 y''(x) + \cdots + a_n x^n y^{(n)}(x) = f(x)$$

is called a **Cauchy–Euler equation**.

MATLAB can solve this type of equation directly with the command *dsolve* or *maple('dsolve')*.

EXERCISE 3-5

Solve the following differential equation:

$$x^3 y'''' + 16x^2 y'' + 79xy' + 125y = 0.$$

```
» pretty(simple(dsolve('x^3*D3y+16*x^2*D2y+79*x*Dy+125*y=0')))

       C1 + C2 sin(3 log(x)) x + C3 cos(3 log(x)) x
       ---------------------------------------------
                            5
                           x
```

The Laplace Transform

Suppose $f(t)$ is a function defined in the interval $(0, \infty)$. The **Laplace transform** of $f(t)$ is the function $F(s)$ defined by:

$$F(s) = L\{f(t)\}(s) = \int_0^\infty e^{-st} f(t) dt.$$

We say that $f(t)$ is the inverse Laplace transform of $F(s)$, so that

$$L^{-1}\{F(s)\}(t) = f(t).$$

MATLAB provides the commands *maple('laplace')* and *maple('invlaplace')* to calculate the Laplace transform and inverse Laplace transform of an expression with respect to a variable. Its syntax is as follows:

> **maple('laplace(expression, t, s)'): This calculates the Laplace transform of a given expression with respect to t. The transformed variable is s.**

> **maple('(expression, s, t) invlaplace'): This computes the inverse Laplace transform of the given expression with respect to s. The inverse variable is t.**

Here are some examples.

```
» pretty(maple('laplace(t^(3/2)-exp(t)+sinh(a*t), t, s)'));
```

$$
3/4 \ \frac{pi^{1/2}}{s^{5/2}} - \frac{1}{s-1} + \frac{a}{s^2-a^2}
$$

```
» pretty(maple('invlaplace(s^2/(s^2+a^2)^(3/2), s, t)'))
```

$$
- t \ BesselJ(1, \ a \ t) \ a + BesselJ(0, \ a \ t)
$$

The Laplace transform and its inverse are used to solve certain differential equations. The method is to calculate the Laplace transform of each term of the equation to obtain a new differential equation, which we then solve. Finally, we find the solution of the original equation by applying the inverse Laplace transform to the solution just found.

MATLAB provides the 'laplace' option in the maple('dsolve') command, which forces the program to solve the differential equation using the Laplace transform method. The syntax is as follows:

```
maple('dsolve(equation, func(var), 'laplace')')
```

EXERCISE 3-6

Solve the differential equation

$$
y'' + 2y' + 4y = x - e^{-x}, \ y(0)=1, \ y'(0)=1
$$

using the Laplace transform method.

First, we calculate the Laplace transform of each side of the differential equation, and we apply the initial conditions.

```
» maple('L:=s->laplace(diff(y(x),x$2)+2*diff(y(x),x)+4*y(x),x,s)');
» pretty(simplify('subs(y(0)=1,(D(y))(0)=1,L(s))'))
```

$$
laplace(y(x), \ x, \ s) \ s - s - 3 + 2 \ laplace(y(x), \ x, \ s) \ s
$$

$$
+ 4 \ laplace(y(x), \ x, \ s)
$$

```
» maple('L1:=s->laplace(x-exp(-x),x,s)');
» pretty(simplify('L1(s)'))
```

$$
\frac{1}{s^2} - \frac{1}{s+1}
$$

We then solve the Laplace transformed differential equation:

```
» pretty(simplify(maple('solve(L(s)=L1(s),laplace(y(x),x,s))')))
```

$$\frac{s^4 \, y(0) + (3\,y(0) + D(y)(0))\,s^3 + (2\,y(0) + D(y)(0) - 1)\,s^2 + s + 1}{s^2\,(s^3 + 3\,s^2 + 6\,s + 4)}$$

Now we substitute the given initial conditions into the solution.

```
» maple('TL:=s->solve(L(s)=L1(s),laplace(y(x),x,s))');
» pretty(simplify('subs(y(0)=1,(D(y))(0)=1,TL(s))'))
```

$$\frac{s^4 + 4\,s^3 + 2\,s^2 + s + 1}{s^2\,(s + 1)\,(s^2 + 2\,s + 4)}$$

This gives the solution of the Laplace transformed equation. To calculate the solution of the original equation we calculate the inverse Laplace transform of the solution obtained in the previous step.

```
» maple('TL0:=s->simplify('subs(y(0)=1,(D(y))(0)=1,TL(s))')');
» solucion=simple(maple('invlaplace(TL0(s),s,x)'));
» pretty(solution)
```

$$1/4\,x - 1/8 - \frac{1}{3\,\exp(x)} + 5/8\,\frac{\sin(3^{1/2}\,x)\,3^{1/2}}{\exp(x)} + \frac{35}{24}\,\frac{\cos(3^{1/2}\,x)}{\exp(x)}$$

This gives the solution of the original differential equation.

We could also have solved it directly via:

```
» pretty(simple(sym(maple('dsolve({diff(y(x),x$2)+2*diff(y(x),x)+4*y(x) = x-exp(-x), y(0)=1,D(y)
(0)=1},y(x),laplace)'))))
```

$$y(x) = 1/4\,x - 1/8 - \frac{1}{3\,\exp(x)} + 5/8\,\frac{\sin(3^{1/2}\,x)\,3^{1/2}}{\exp(x)} + \frac{35}{24}\,\frac{\cos(3^{1/2}\,x)}{\exp(x)}$$

Orthogonal Polynomials

Two functions $f(x)$ and $g(x)$ are said to be **orthogonal** on an interval $[a, b]$ if their inner product is 0, i.e. if

$$\int_a^b f(x)g(x)dx = 0.$$

An example of an orthogonal family of functions (i.e. such that any two distinct functions in the family are orthogonal) is given by:

$$f_n(x) = \sin(nx) \text{ and } g_n(x) = \cos(nx), n = 1, 2, 3, \ldots, \text{ in the interval } [-\pi, \pi].$$

MATLAB provides a broad list of orthogonal polynomials, which are very useful in solving certain non-linear differential equations of higher order. The functions that allow us to work with these polynomials are the following:

T(n,x), **Chebychev polynomials of the first kind.**

U(n,x), **Chebychev polynomials of the second kind.**

P(n,x), **Legendre polynomials.**

H(n,x), **Hermite polynomials.**

L(n,x), **Laguerre polynomials.**

L(n,a,x), **Generalized Laguerre polynomials.**

P(n,a,b,x), **Jacobi polynomials.**

G(n,m,x), **Gegenbauer polynomials.**

Now let us look at their relationship to differential equations. It is precisely this relationship which allows us to find solutions of some non-linear equations of higher order. To use these functions we first need to run *maple('with orthopoly')*.

Chebychev Polynomials of the First and Second Kind

The Chebychev polynomials of the first kind are defined as the solutions $T_n(x)$ of the differential equation:

$$\left(1-x^2\right)y'' - x'y + n^2y = 0, n = 0,1,2,\ldots$$

Their orthogonality is given by the weighted inner product:

$$\int_{-1}^1 \frac{T_m(x)T_n(x)}{\sqrt{\left(1-x^2\right)}} dx = 0, m \neq n.$$

The Chebychev polynomials of the second kind $U_n(x)$ are special cases of the Jacobi polynomials (see below) with $a = b = 1/2$. They satisfy the orthogonality relationship:

$$\int_{-1}^1 U_n(x)U_m(x)\left(1-x^2\right)^{\frac{1}{2}} dx = 0, m \neq n.$$

Legendre Polynomials

The Legendre polynomials $P_n(x)$ are solutions of the Legendre differential equation:

$$(1-x^2)y'' - 2x'y + n(n+1)y = 0.$$

Their orthogonality is given by the relation

$$\int_{-1}^{1} P_n(x)P_m(x)dx = 0, \; m \neq n.$$

Associated Legendre Polynomials

The solutions of the differential equation

$$(1-x^2)y'' - 2x'y + \left[n(n+1) - \frac{m^2}{1-x^2}\right]y = 0$$

are called associated Legendre polynomials.
    Their orthogonality is given by the relation

$$\int_{-1}^{1} P_k^m P_l^m dx = \frac{2(l+m)!}{(2l+1)(l-m)!}\delta_{k,l}$$

where $d_{k,l}$ is the Kronecker delta.

Hermite Polynomials

The solutions $H_n(x)$ of the Hermite differential equation

$$y'' - 2x'y + 2ny = 0$$

are known as Hermite polynomials.
    Their orthogonality is given by the weighted inner product:

$$\int_{-\infty}^{\infty} H_n(x)H_m(x)e^{-x^2}dx = 0, \; m \neq n.$$

Generalized Laguerre Polynomials

The solutions $L_n(x)$ of the general Laguerre differential equation

$$xy'' + (a+1-x)y' + ny = 0$$

are known as generalized Laguerre polynomials.
    Their orthogonality is given by the weighted inner product:

$$\int_{0}^{\infty} L_n(x)L_m(x)x^a e^{-x}dx = 0, \; m \neq n.$$

Laguerre Polynomials

The solutions of the Laguerre differential equation

$$x''y + (1-x)y' + ny = 0$$

are known as Laguerre polynomials. This is the particular case $a = 0$ of the generalized Laguerre polynomials.

Jacobi Polynomials

The solutions of the Jacobi differential equation

$$(1-x^2)y'' + (b-a-(a+b+2)x)y' + n(n+a+b+1)y = 0$$

are known as Jacobi polynomials.

Their orthogonality is given by the weighted inner product:

$$\int_{-1}^{1} P_n(x)P_m(x)(1-x)^a(1+x)^b \, dx = 0, \, m \neq n.$$

Gegenbauer Polynomials

The Gegenbauer polynomial $G(n, a, x)$ is defined as follows:

$$G(n,a,x) = \frac{\Gamma\left(a + \frac{1}{2}\right)\Gamma(n+2a)}{(-2)^n \, n! \, \Gamma(2a)\Gamma\left(a+n+\frac{1}{2}\right)(1-x^2)^{a-\frac{1}{2}}} \left(\frac{d}{dx}\right)^n (1-x^2)^{n+a-\frac{1}{2}}$$

The solutions of the Gegenbauer differential equation

$$(1-x^2)y'' + (2a+1)xy' + n(n+2a)y = 0$$

are known as Gegenbauer polynomials.

Their orthogonality is given by the weighted inner product:

$$\int_{-1}^{1} G(n,a,x)G(m,a,x)(1-x^2)^{a-\frac{1}{2}} \, dx = 0 \, m \neq n.$$

EXERCISE 3-7

Find the solutions to the following differential equations:

$$(1-x^2)y'' - xy' + 49y = 0,$$
$$(1-x^2)y'' - 2xy' + 42y = 0,$$
$$y'' - 2xy' + 10y = 0,$$
$$xy'' + (1-x)y' + 5y = 0.$$

```
» pretty(simple(maple('T(7,x)')))
```

```
    7          5          3
64 x   - 112 x   + 56 x   - 7 x
```

```
» pretty(simple(maple('P(6,x)')))
```

```
231  6    315  4    105  2
--- x   - --- x   + --- x   - 5/16
 16        16        16
```

```
» pretty(simple(maple('H(5,x)')))
```

```
    5          3
32 x   - 160 x   + 120 x
```

```
» pretty(simple(maple('L(5,x)')))
```

```
       2       3         4          5
1-5 x + 5 x  - 5/3 x + 5/24 x  - 1/120 x
```

Bessel and Airy Functions

The linearly independent solutions of the following second order differential equation are called **Airy functions**:

$$y'' - xy = 0 \text{ (Airy equation)}$$

The linearly independent solutions of the following second order differential equation are called **Bessel functions**:

$$y'' + \frac{y'}{x} + \left(k^2 - \frac{n^2}{x^2}\right)y = 0 \text{ (Bessel equation)}$$

The linearly independent solutions of the following differential equation are called **modified Bessel functions**:

$$y'' + \frac{y'}{x} - \left(k^2 + n^2 x\right)y = 0 \text{ (modified Bessel equation)}$$

MATLAB implements the following related functions:

Ai(z) and Bi(z) are the linearly independent solutions of the Airy differential equation.

BesselJ(n,z) and BesselY(n,z) are the linearly independent solutions of the Bessel differential equation.

BesselI(n,z) and BesselK(n,z) are the linearly independent solutions of the modified Bessel differential equation.

EXERCISE 3-8

Find the solutions of the differential equation

$$x^2 y'' + xy' + \left(x^2 - \frac{1}{4} \right) y = 0.$$

The equation is the Bessel differential equation with n = 1/2. We obtain two linearly independent solutions as follows:

```
» pretty(simple(maple('BesselJ(1/2,x)')))

       1/2
      2    sin(x)
      ----------
       1/2   1/2
      pi    x
```

```
» pretty(simple(maple('BesselY(1/2,x)')))

      1/2
     2       cos(x)
   - -----------
      1/2  1/2
     x    pi
```

CHAPTER 4

■ ■ ■

Differential Equations Via Approximation Methods

Higher Order Equations and Approximation Methods

When the known algebraic methods for solving differential equations and systems of differential equations offer no solution, we usually resort to methods of approximation. The approximation methods can involve both symbolic and numerical work. The symbolic approach yields approximate algebraic solutions, and its most representative technique is the Taylor series method. The numerical approach yields a solution in the form of a finite set of solution points, to which a curve can be fitted by various algebraic methods (interpolation, regression,…). This curve will be an approximate solution of the differential equation. Among the most common numerical methods is the Runge–Kutta method.

Approximation methods are most commonly employed to find the solution of equations and systems of differential equations of order and degree greater than one, where the exact solution cannot be obtained by other methods.

The Taylor Series Method

This method provides approximate polynomial solutions of general differential equations, and is based on the Taylor series expansion of functions. MATLAB offers the option '*series*' for the command *maple('dsolve')*, which allows you to solve equations by this method. Its syntax is as follows:

```
maple('dsolve(equation, func(var), 'series'))
```

There is also the command *maple('powsolve')*, which gives a power series solution of linear differential equations, and whose syntax is as follows:

```
maple('powseries [powsolve](equation, cond1,...,condn) ')
```

Using the command *maple('convert(polynom)')* you can convert a complicated solution to a polynomial in powers of the variable.

EXERCISE 4-1

Solve the following two equations by the Taylor series method:

$$4x^2y'' + 4xy' + (x^2 - 1)y = 0,$$

$$yy'' + (y')^2 + 1 = 0, \text{ with the initial conditions } y(0) + 1 \text{ and } y'(0) = 1.$$

» pretty(simple(maple('dsolve(4 * x ^ 2 * diff(y(x), x$ 2) + 4 * x * diff(y(x), x) +(x ^ 2-1)
* y(x) = 0 y(x), series)')))

```
                   2        4       6                    6
y(x) = (_C1 x(1 - 1/24 x  + 1/1920 x  + O(x )) + _C2 log(x)(O(x ))

               2        4       6    /  1/2
    + _C2(1 - 1/8 x  + 1/384 x + O(x ))) /  x
```

» pretty(simplify(maple('convert(_C1 * x ^(1/2) *(1-1 / 24 * x ^ 2 + 1/1920 * x ^ 4 + O(x^6))
+ _C2 *(1/x ^(1/2) * log(x) *(O(x^6)) + 1/x ^(1/2) *(1-1 / 8 * x ^ 2 + 1/384 * x ^ 4 + O(x^6))),
polynom)')))

```
                    3        5            6
    1/1920(1920 _C1 x - 80 x _C1 + _C1 x + 1920 _C1 x o(x))

                6                       2        4
    + 1920 _C2 log(x) o(x) + 1920 _C2 - 240 _C2 x + 5_C2 x

              6    1/2
    (+1920 _C2 o(x)) / x
```

» pretty(maple('dsolve({y(x) * diff(y(x), x$ 2) + diff(y(x), x) ^ 2 + 1 = 0, y(0) = 1,
D(y)(0) = 1}, y(x), series)'))

```
                2    3     4        5        6
    y(x) = 1 + x - x  + x  - 3/2 x  + 5/2 x  + O(x )
```

EXERCISE 4-2

Solve the following two systems of equations using the Taylor series method:

$$x'' + y' - 4x + 12 = 0$$
$$y'' - 10x - y + 7 = 0$$
$$x(0) = y(0) = x'(0) = y'(0) = 1$$

and

$$x'' + 2x' + 2y' + 3z' = 1$$
$$y' + z' - x = 0$$
$$x' + z = 0.$$

» **pretty(simple(maple('dsolve({diff(x(t), t$ 2) + diff(y(t), t) - 4 * x + 12 = 0, diff(y(t), t$ 2) - 10 * diff(x(t), t) y(t) + 7 = 0, x(0) = 1, y(0) = 1, D(0) = 1, D(x)(y)(0) = 1}, {x(t), y(t)}, series)')))**

$$\{y(t) = 1 + t + 2\ t^2 + (-43/2 + 20/3\ x)\ t^3 - 3/2\ t^4 + (\frac{387}{40} - 3\ x)\ t^5 + O(t^6),$$

$$x(t) = 1 + t + (-13/2 + 2\ x)\ t^2 - 2/3\ t^3 + (43/8 - 5/3\ x)\ t^4 + 3/10\ t^5 + O(t^6)\}$$

» **pretty(simple(maple('dsolve({diff(x(t),t$2)+2*diff(x(t),t)+2*diff(y(t),t)+ 3*diff(z(t),t)+x(t)=1,diff(y(t),t)+diff(z(t),t)-x(t)=0,diff(x(t),t)+z(t)=0}, {x(t),y(t),z(t)}, series)')))**

$$\{x(t) = x(0) + D(x)(0)\ t + (-D(x)(0) - 1/2\ x(0) + 1/2)\ t^2$$
$$+ (1/2\ D(x)(0) + 1/3\ x(0) - 1/3)\ t^3 + (-1/6\ D(x)(0) - 1/8\ x(0) + 1/8)\ t^4$$
$$+ (1/24\ D(x)(0) + 1/30\ x(0) - 1/30)\ t^5 + O(t^6),$$

$$z(t) = z(0) + x(0)\ t + 1/2\ D(x)(0)\ t^2 + (-1/3\ D(x)(0) - 1/6\ x(0) + 1/6)\ t^3$$
$$+ (1/8\ D(x)(0) + 1/12\ x(0) - 1/12)\ t^4$$
$$+ (-1/30\ D(x)(0) - 1/40\ x(0) + 1/40)\ t^5 + O(t^6),$$

$$y(t) = y(0) + x(0)\ t + 1/2\ D(x)(0)\ t^2 + (-1/3\ D(x)(0) - 1/6\ x(0) + 1/6)\ t^3$$
$$+ (1/8\ D(x)(0) + 1/12\ x(0) - 1/12)\ t^4$$
$$+ (-1/30\ D(x)(0) - 1/40\ x(0) + 1/40)\ t^5 + O(t^6) \quad \}$$

$$\}$$

The Runge–Kutta Method

The Runge-Kutta method gives a set of data points to which you can fit a curve, approximating the solution of a differential equation. Maple provides the option *numeric* for the command *maple('solve')* which enables the calculation of approximate numerical solutions of differential equations. Its syntax is:

```
maple('dsolve(equation, func(var), 'numeric'))
```

EXERCISE 4-3

Solve the following equation using the Runge–Kutta method:

$$3(y'')^2 = y''' \, y' \text{ with the initial conditions } y'(0) = y''(0) = 1.$$

» maple('f: = dsolve({3 * diff(y(x), x$ 2) ^ 2 = diff(y(x), x$ 3) * diff(y(x), x), y(0) = 1/2, D(y)(0) = 1,(D@@2)(y)(0) = 1}, y(x), numeric)')

ans =

f := proc(x) `dsolve/numeric/result2`(x,3879004,[3]) end

Now, in order to graph the solution, we calculate various points of the solution function *f* generated above (see Figure 4-1).

» [maple('f(-0.3)'),maple('f(-0.2)'),maple('f(-0.1)'),maple('f(0)'), maple('f(0.1)'), maple('f(0.2)'),maple('f(0.3)')]

ans =

{x = -.3,y(x) = .2350889359260396}{y(x) = .3167840433732281, x = -.2}
{y(x) = .4045548849869109, x = -.1}{y(x) = .5000000000000000, x = 0}
{x = .1, y(x) = .6055728090006967}{y(x) = .7254033307597474, x = .2}
{y(x) = .8675444679682489, x = .3000000000000000}

» y = [.2350889359260396,.3167840433732281,.4045548849869109,.5,.6055728090006967,
.7254033307597474,.8675444679682489];
» plot((-0.3:.1:0.3), y)

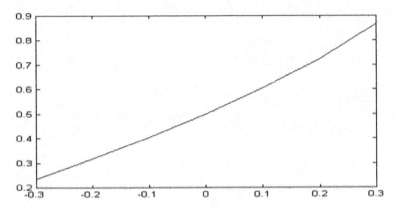

Figure 4-1.

We find the degree 2 polynomial which is the best fit to the set of solution points. The equation of this parabola will be an approximate solution of the differential equation.

» pretty(vpa(poly2sym(polyfit((-0.3:.1:0.3),y,2))))

2
.5747427827483573 *x* + 1.041293962469090 *x* +.4991457846921903

This yields a degree 2 polynomial approximation to the solution *y* (*x*) of the equation.

CHAPTER 5

■ ■ ■

Systems of Differential Equations and Finite Difference Equations

Systems of Linear Homogeneous Equations with Constant Coefficients

MATLAB can solve this type of system directly, simply by using the command *dsolve* or *maple('dsolve')* with the familiar syntax.

A system of differential equations, written as $X'(t)=AX(t)$ has a general solution of the form:

$$X(t)=\sum_{i=1}^{n} c_i V_i e^{\lambda_i t}$$

where the eigenvalues $\{\lambda_k\}$ ($K=1,2,\ldots n$) corresponding to the eigenvectors $\{V_k\}$ of the matrix of the system are all assumed to be different.

If an eigenvalue λ_k is a complex number $a_k+b_k i$, then it generates the following component of the overall solution:

$$C_{k1} W_{k1} e^{\lambda_k t} + C_{k2} W_{k2} e^{\lambda_k t}$$

where:

$$W_{k1} = \frac{1}{2}(V_k+\bar{V}_k)\cos(b_k t)+\frac{i}{2}(V_k+\bar{V}_k)\sin(b_k t),$$

$$W_{k2} = \frac{i}{2}(V_k+\bar{V}_k)\cos(b_k t)+\frac{1}{2}(V_k+\bar{V}_k)\sin(b_k t).$$

Here $\bar{V}_k$ is the eigenvector corresponding to the eigenvalue λ_k and $\bar{V}_k$ is its conjugate.

If there is an eigenvalue λ_i of multiplicity $m>1$, then it will generate a portion of the general solution of the form:

$$c_i e^{\lambda_i t} V_i + c_{i+1} t e^{\lambda_i t} V_{i+1} + c_{i+2} t^2 e^{\lambda_i t} V_{i+2} + \ldots + c_{i+k} t^k e^{\lambda_i t} V_k.$$

EXERCISE 5-1

Solve the following system of equations:

$$x'=-5x+3y,$$
$$y'=-2x-10y.$$

» **pretty(dsolve('Dx=-5*x+3*y,Dy=-2*x-10*y','t'))**

y(t) = C1 exp(- 7 t) + C2 exp(- 8 t),

x(t) = - 3/2 C1 exp(- 7 t) - C2 exp(- 8 t)

You can also use the following syntax:

» **pretty(maple('dsolve({diff(x(t), t) =-5 * x(t) + 3 * y(t), diff(y(t), t) =-2 * x(t) - 10 * y(t)}, {x(t), y(t)})'))**

{y(t) = _C1 exp(- 7 t) + _C2 exp(- 8 t),

x(t) = - 3/2 _C1 exp(- 7 t) - _C2 exp(- 8 t)}

Systems of Linear Non-Homogeneous Equations with Constant Coefficients

Now let us consider systems of non-homogeneous differential equations with constant coefficients of the form $X' = AX + F(t)$.

The general solution of the homogeneous system $X' = AX$ takes the form $X = \phi(t)C$. A particular solution of the non-homogeneous system is:

$$X_p = \phi(t) \int \phi^{-1}(t) F(t) dt.$$

The general solution of the non-homogeneous system will be $X = \phi(t)C + X_p$, which is, using the previous expression:

$$X = \phi(t)C + \phi(t) \int \phi^{-1}(t) F(t) dt.$$

This method is a generalization to systems of equations of the method of variation of parameters for simple equations.

MATLAB can solve such systems of equations directly with the command *dsolve* or *maple('dsolve')*, provided the integrals that appear in the solution can be evaluated.

EXERCISE 5-2

Solve the following system of equations:

$$x'-y'=e^{-t}$$
$$y'+5x+2y=\sin(3+t)$$

with initial conditions $x(0) = x0$ and $y(0) = y0$.

» pretty(simple(dsolve('Dx-Dy = exp(-t), Dy+5 * x + 2 * y =sin(3 + t) ', ' x(0) = xo,
y(0) = yo ', 't ')))

y(t) = 7/50 sin(3) cos(t) + 7/50 cos(3) sin(t) + 5/6 exp(-t)

+ 1/50 sin(3) sin(t) - 1/50 cos(3) cos(t) - 5/7 + 5/7 yo - 5/7 xo

+(-7/50 sin(3) + 2/7 yo + 1/50 cos(3) - 5/42 + 5/7 xo) exp(-7t)

Finite Difference Equations

The MATLAB function *maple('rsolve')* enables you to solve finite difference equations and recurrence equations in general. Its syntax is:

```
maple('rsolve({equation, initial_conditions}, function)')
```

EXERCISE 5-3

Find the solutions of the following recurrence equations:

$$y_{m+1}=my_m+(m+1)!\quad y_1=2,$$
$$y_{2n}=4y_n+5\quad y_1=a,$$
$$y_{n+2}-3y_{n+1}+2y_n=4^n\quad y_0=y_1=1.$$

» pretty(maple('rsolve({y(m + 1) = m * y(m) +(m + 1)!, y(1) = 2}, y)'))

```
 2
1/2 GAMMA(m)(m + m + 2).
```

» pretty(maple('rsolve({y(2*n) = 4 *y(n) + 5, y(1) = a}, y)'))

```
                                 log(n)
                                 ------ + 1
             2    2              log(2)
          a n  + n (- 20/3(1/4)            + 5/3)
```

» pretty(maple('rsolve({y(n + 2) - 3 * y(n + 1) + 2 *y(n) = 4 ^ n, y(0) = 1 y(1) = 1}, y)'))

```
 n        n
4/3 - 1/2 2 + 1/6 4
```

EXERCISE 5-4

Find the general term of the sequences of real numbers defined by the following recurrence laws:

$$x_n - n_{xm} * x_n x_{n+1} = x_{n+1} \quad x_0 = 1,$$
$$y_{n+2} - 2y_{n+1} + 5y_n = \cos(3n) \quad y_0 = y_1 = 1$$

```
» pretty(maple('rsolve({x(n) - n *x(n)  * x(n + 1) = x(n + 1),
x(0) = 1}, x)'))
```

```
        2
   ----------
      2
   n - n + 2
```

```
» maple('rsolve({x(n + 2) - 2 * x(n + 1) + 5 * x(n) = cos(3*n), x(0) = 1, x(1) = 1}, x)')
```

ans =

+10*cos(n-3)^3*cos(1)^2+10*cos(n-3)^3*cos(3)^2-72*cos(n-3)^3*cos(3)-72*cos(n-3)^3*cos(1)
-49*cos(n-4)^3* 1/2*(1-2*i)^n+1/2*(1+2*i)^n+(-39*cos(n-2)^3+22*cos(n-5)^3-19*cos(n-4)^3+32*
cos(n-3)^3-25*cos(n-2)^3*cos(1)-25*cos(n-2)^3*cos(3)+100*cos(n-2)^3*cos(1)^2+100*cos(n-2)^3*
cos(3)^2cos(1) + 120 * cos(n-4) ^ 3 * cos(3) ^ 2 + 120 * cos(n-4) ^ 3 * cos(1) ^ 2-49 *
cos(n-4) ^ 3 * cos(3)-60*cos(n-5)^3*cos(3)-60*cos(n-5)^3*cos(1)+169*cos(n-2)^3*cos(1)*
cos(3)-120*cos(n-2)^3 * cos(3) * cos(1) ^ 2-120 * cos(n-2) ^ 3 * cos(3) ^ 2 * cos(1) - 290 *
cos(n-3) ^ 3 * cos(3) ^ 2 * cos(1) + 200 * cos(n-3) ^ 3 * cos(3) ^ 2 * cos(1) ^ 2 + 208 *
cos(n-3) ^3 * cos(1) * cos(3) - 290 * cos(n-3) ^ 3 * cos(3) * cos(1)^2-100*cos(n-4)^3*cos(3)*
cos(1)^2+265*cos(n-4)^3*cos(1)*cos(3)-100*cos(n-4)^3 * cos(3) ^ 2 * cos(1) + 50 * cos(n-5) ^ 3
* cos(1) * cos(3) + 100 * cos(n-2) ^ 3 * cos(3) ^ 2 * cos(1) ^ 2) /(25 * cos(3) ^ 2 + 36 *
cos(1) * cos(3) - 30 * cos(3) - 30 * cos(3) ^ 2 * cos(1) + 25 * cos(1) ^ 2-30 * cos())1)-30
* cos(3) * cos(1) ^ 2 + 25 + 25 * cos(3) ^ 2 * cos(1) ^ 2) + 1/4 *(- 30 * i *(1+2*i) ^ n-35
*(1-2*i) ^ n * cos(3) ^ 2-+27*(1-2*i)^n*cos(1)-25*(1-2*i)^n*cos(1)^2-35*(1+2*i)^n*cos(3)^
2-37*i*(1-2*i)^n*cos(3)-25*(1+2*i)^n*cos(1)^2+21*(1-2*i)^n*cos(3)^2*cos(1)+23*(1-2*i)^n*
cos(3)*cos(1)^)2-20*(1-2*i)^n*cos(3)^2*cos(1)^2+25*i*(1-2*i)^n*cos(3)^2+15*i*(1-2*i)^n*
cos(1)^2-20*(1+2*i)^n * cos(3) ^ 2 * cos(1) ^ 2-15 * i *(1+2*i) ^ n * cos(1) ^ 2 + 37 * i
*(1+2*i) ^ n * cos(3) + 39 * i *(1+2*i) ^ n * cos(1) - 39 * i *(1-2*i) ^ n * cos(1) + 21
*(1+2*i) ^ n * cos(3) ^ 2 * cos(1) + 41 *(1+2*)(i) ^ n * cos(3) + 27 *(1+2*i) ^ n * cos(1)
+ 48 * i *(1-2*i) ^ n * cos(1) * cos(3) + 10 * i *(1-2*i) ^ n * cos(3) ^ 2 * cos(1) ^ 2-25 *
i *(1+2*i) ^ n * cos(3) ^ 2 + 19 * i *(1+2*i) ^ n * cos(3) * cos(1) ^ 2-48 * i *(1+2*i) ^ n *
cos(1) * cos(3) + 33 * i *(1+2*i) ^ n * cos(3) ^ 2 * cos(1) - 24 *(1+2*i) ^ n * cos(1) * cos(3)
+ 23 *)(1+2*i)^n*cos(3)*cos(1)^2-40*(1-2*i)^n-40*(1+2*i)^n+41*(1-2*i)^n*cos(3)-10*i*(1+2*i)^n*
cos(3)^2*cos(1)^2-33*i*(1-2*i)^n*cos(3)^2*cos(1)+30*i*(1-2*i)^n-24*(1-2*i)^n*cos(1)*
cos(3)-19*i*(1-2*i)^n*cos(3) * cos(1) ^ 2) /(5 * cos(1) ^ 2-6 * cos(1) + 5) /(5-6 * cos(3)
+ 5 * cos(3) ^ 2) - 3 /2*(-2*cos(n-2)*cos(1)-2*cos(n-2)+10*cos(n-2)*cos(1)^2-5*cos(n-3)*
cos(1)+cos(n-3))/(5*cos(1)^2-6*cos(1)+5)-3/8*(i*(1-2*i)^n*cos)1)^2-2*(1-2*i)^n*cos(1)^2-4*
i*(1-2*i)^n*cos(1)+3*i*(1-2*i)^n-4*(1-2*i)^n+2*(1-2*i)^n*cos(1)-2*(1+2*i)^n*cos(1)^2-i*
(1+2*i)^n*cos(1)^2+4*i*(1+2*i)^n*cos(1)-4*(1+2*i)^n-3*i*(1+2*i)^n+2*(1+2*i)^n*cos(1))/
(5*cos(1)^2-6*cos(1)+5)

Now we try to simplify the above non-trivial result.

» pretty(simple(maple('evalf(rsolve({x(n+2)-2*x(n+1)+5*x(n)=cos(3*n), x(0)=1,x(1)=1},x))')))

.4373424525 exp((.8047189562 - 1.107148718 I) n)

+ .4373424525 exp((.8047189562 + 1.107148718 I) n)

$$- .9160727930 \; cos(n - 3.)^3 + .4362567143 \; cos(n - 5.)^3$$

$$+ .1725076052 \; cos(n - 2.)^3 - .1986350636 \; cos(n - 4.)^3$$

- .06265675740 I exp((.8047189562 + 1.107148718 I) n)

+ .06265675750 I exp((.8047189562 - 1.107148718 I) n)

+ .7931668115 cos(n - 3.) + .07520876265 cos(n - 2.)

Partial Differential Equations

MATLAB implements several commands which can be used when working with partial differential equations, all of which require the prior use of the *maple* command. We have:

> **pdesolve (pdeqn, fnc (var 1,.., varn)):** This solves the partial differential equation pdeqn for the function fnc (var1,.., varn).

> **pdesolve (exprpd, fnc (var1,.., varn)):** This solves the partial differential equation exprpd=0.

> **DEtools[PDEchangecoords] (pdeqn, [varind, 1,.., varind, n], option):** This converts the partial differential equation pdeqn in the independent variables varind1,.., varindn to the new coordinate system defined by the option. The possible two-dimensional coordinate systems are bipolar, cardoid, cassinian, elliptic, hyperbolic, invcassinian, invelliptic, logarithmic, logcosh, maxwell, parabolic, polar, rose and tangent. For three dimensions possible systems include, among others, bispherical, cardoidal, conical, cylindrical, ellipsoidal, paraboloidal, sixsphere, spherical and toroidal.

> **DEtools [PDEchangecoords] (pdeqn, [va1,.., van], option, [vn1, .., vnn]):** This converts the partial differential equation pdeqn to the specified new coordinate system in the given independent variables.

> **DEtools[PDEchangecoords] ({pdeqn1, .., pdeqnm}, [varind1, .., varindn], option):** This converts the given system of partial differential equations to the specified new coordinate system in the given independent variables.

EXAMPLES:

» **pretty(sym(maple('pdesolve(diff(f(x,y),x,x)+5*diff(f(x,y),x,y)=3, f(x,y))')))**

$$f(x, y) = 3/2 \; x^2 + \_F1(y) + \_F2(y - 5 \; x)$$

» **pretty(sym(maple('pdesolve(3*diff(g(x,y),x)+7*diff(g(x,y),x,y)=x*y, g(x,y)) ')))**

$$g(x, y) = 1/6 \; x^2 \; y - 7/18 \; x^2 + \_F1(y) + \exp(- \; 3/7 \; y) \; \_F2(x)$$

» **pretty(sym(maple('pdesolve(diff(h(x,y),x,x)-diff(h(x,y),y,y)=0, h(x,y)) ')))**

$$h(x, y) = \_F1(y + x) + \_F2(y - x)$$

» **pretty(sym(maple('pdesolve(y*diff(U(x,y),x)+x*diff(U(x,y),y)=0, U(x,y)) ')))**

$$U(x, y) = \_F1(-x^2 + y^2).$$

■ ■ ■

CHAPTER 6

Numerical Calclus with MATLAB. Applications to Differential Equations

MATLAB and Programming

MATLAB can be used as a high-level programming language including data structures, functions, instructions for flow control, management of inputs/outputs and even object-oriented programming.

MATLAB programs are usually written in files called M-files. An M-file is nothing more than a MATLAB code (*script*) that executes a series of commands or functions that accept arguments and produce an output. The M-files are created using the text editor.

Text Editor

The *Editor/Debugger* is activated by clicking on the *create a new M-file* button ▢ in the MATLAB desktop or by selecting *File* ➤ *New* ➤ *M-file* in the MATLAB desktop (Figure 6-1) or Command Window (Figure 6-2). The *Editor/Debugger* opens a file in which we create the M-file, i.e. a blank file into which we will write MATLAB programming code (Figure 6-3). You can open an existing M-file using *File* ➤ *Open* on the MATLAB desktop (Figure 6-1) or, alternatively, you can use the command *Open* in the Command Window (Figure 6-2). You can also open the *Editor/Debugger* by right-clicking on the *Current Directory* window and choosing *New* ➤ *M-file* from the resulting pop-up menu (Figure 6-4). Using the menu option *Open*, you can open an existing M-file. You can open several M-files simultaneously, each of which will appear in a different window.

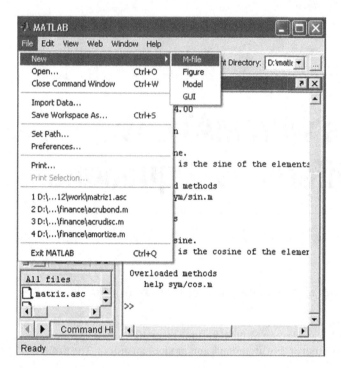

Figure 6-1.

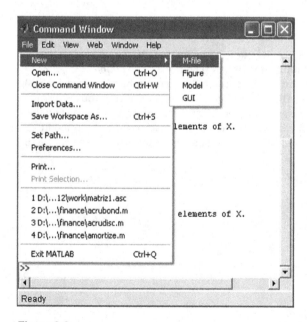

Figure 6-2.

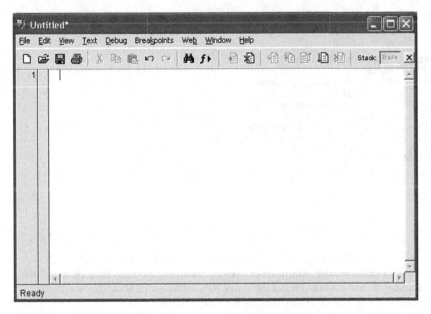

Figure 6-3.

Figure 6-4.

Figure 6-5 shows the functions of the icons in the Editor/Debugger.

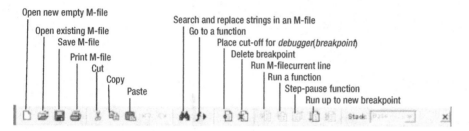

Figure 6-5.

Scripts

Scripts are the simplest possible M-files. A script has no input or output arguments. It simply consists of instructions that MATLAB executes sequentially and that could also be submitted in a sequence in the Command Window. Scripts operate with existing data on the workspace or new data created by the script. Any variable that is used by a script will remain in the workspace and can be used in further calculations after the end of the script.

Below is an example of a script that generates several curves in polar form, representing flower petals. Once the syntax of the script has been entered into the editor (Figure 6-6), it is stored in the work library (*work*) and simultaneously executes by clicking the button ⬜ or by selecting the option *Save and run* from the *Debug* menu (or pressing F5). To move from one chart to the next press ENTER.

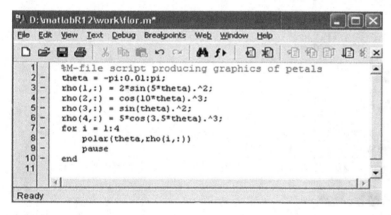

Figure 6-6.

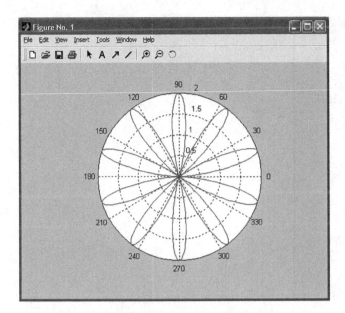

Figure 6-7.

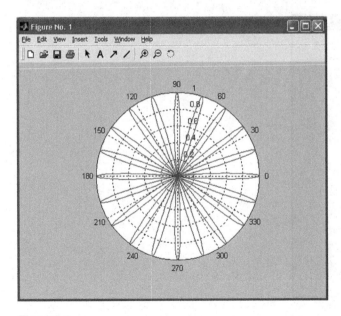

Figure 6-8.

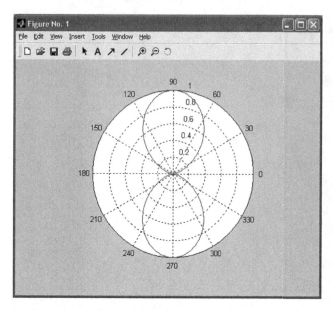

Figure 6-9.

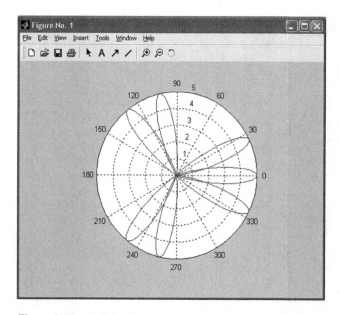

Figure 6-10.

Functions and M-Files. Function, Eval and Feval

We already know that MATLAB has a wide variety of functions that can be used in everyday work with the program. But, in addition, the program also offers the possibility of custom defined functions. The most common way to define a function is to write its definition to a text file, called an M-file, which will be permanent and will therefore enable the function to be used whenever required.

MATLAB is usually used in *command mode* (or *interactive mode*), in which case a command is written in a single line in the Command Window and is immediately processed. But MATLAB also allows the implementation of sets of commands in *batch* mode, in which case a sequence of commands can be submitted which were previously written in a file. This file (M-file) must be stored on disk with the extension ".*m*" in the MATLAB subdirectory, using any ASCII editor or by selecting *M-file New* from the *File* menu in the top menu bar, which opens a text editor that will allow you to write command lines and save the file with a given name. Selecting *M-File Open* from the *File* menu in the top menu bar allows you to edit any pre-existing M-file.

To run an M-file simply type its name (without extension) in interactive mode into the Command Window and press *Enter*. MATLAB sequentially interprets all commands and statements of the M-file line by line and executes them. Normally the literal commands that MATLAB is performing do not appear on screen, except when the command *echo on* is active and only the results of successive executions of the interpreted commands are displayed. Normally, work in batch mode is useful when automating large scale tedious processes which, if done manually, would be prone to mistakes. You can enter explanatory text and comments into M-files by starting each line of the comment with the symbol %. The *help* command can be used to display comments made in a particular M-file.

The command *function* allows the definition of functions in MATLAB, making it one of the most useful applications of M-files. The syntax of this command is as follows:

```
function output_parameters = function_name (input_parameters)
the function body
```

Once the function has been defined, it is stored in an M-file for later use. It is also useful to enter some explanatory text in the syntax of the function (using %), which can be accessed later by using the *help* command.

When there is more than one output parameter, they are placed between square brackets and separated by commas. If there is more than one input parameter, they are separated by commas. The body of the function is the syntax that defines it, and should include commands or instructions that assign values to output parameters. Each command or instruction of the body often appears in a line that ends either with a comma or, when variables are being defined, by a semicolon (in order to avoid duplication of outputs when executing the function). The function is stored in the M-file named *function_name.m*.

Let us define the function *fun1(x)* = $x ^ 3 - 2x + \cos(x)$, creating the corresponding M-file *fun1.m*. To define this function in MATLAB select *M-file New* from the *File* menu in the top menu bar (or click the button in the MATLAB tool bar). This opens the *MATLAB Editor/Debugger* text editor that will allow us to insert command lines defining the function, as shown in Figure 6-11.

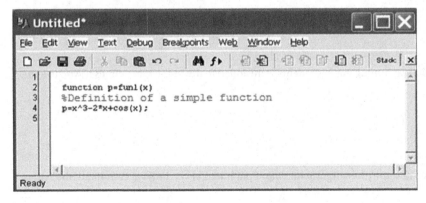

Figure 6-11.

To permanently save this code in MATLAB select the *Save* option from the *File* menu at the top of the *MATLAB Editor/Debugger*. This opens the *Save* dialog of Figure 6-12, which we use to save our function with the desired name and in the subdirectory indicated as a path in the *file name* field. Alternatively you can click on the button 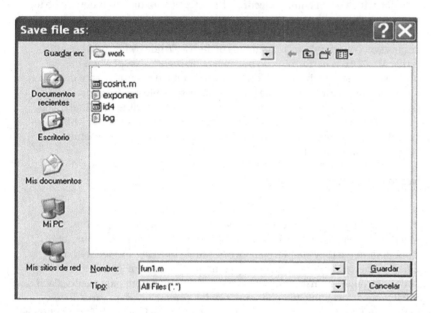 or select *Save and run* from the *Debug* menu. Functions should be saved using a file name equal to the name of the function and in MATLAB's default work subdirectory *C: \MATLAB6p1\work*.

Figure 6-12.

Once a function has been defined and saved in an M-file, it can be used from the Command Window. For example, to find the value of the function at $3\pi/2$ we write in the Command Window:

>> fun1(3*pi/2)

ans =

95.2214

For help on the previous function (assuming that comments were added to the M-file that defines it) you use the command *help*, as follows:

>> help fun1(x)

A simple function definition

A function can also be evaluated at some given arguments (input parameters) via the *feval* command, the syntax of which is as follows:

feval ('F', arg1, arg1,..., argn)

This evaluates the function F (the M-file F.m) at the specified arguments arg1, arg2,..., argn.

As an example we build an M-file named *equation2.m* which contains the function equation2, whose arguments are the three coefficients of the quadratic equation $ax^2 + bx + c = 0$ and whose outputs are the two solutions (Figure 6-13).

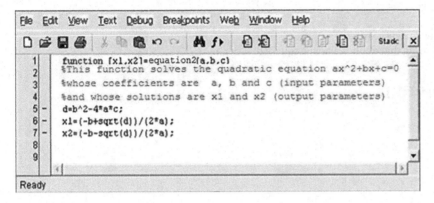

File Edit View Text Debug Breakpoints Web Window Help

```
1   function [x1,x2]=equation2(a,b,c)
2   %This function solves the quadratic equation ax^2+bx+c=0
3   %whose coefficients are  a, b and c (input parameters)
4   %and whose solutions are x1 and x2 (output parameters)
5 - d=b^2-4*a*c;
6 - x1=(-b+sqrt(d))/(2*a);
7 - x2=(-b-sqrt(d))/(2*a);
8
9
```

Ready

Figure 6-13.

Now if we want to solve the equation $x^2 + 2x + 3 = 0$ using *feval*, we write the following in the Command Window:

```
>> [x 1, x 2] = feval('equation2',1,2,3)

x 1 =

-1.0000 + 1. 4142i

x 2 =

-1.0000 - 1. 4142i
```

The quadratic equation can also be solved as follows:

```
>> [x 1, x 2] = equation2 (1,2,3)

x 1 =

  -1.0000 + 1. 4142i

x 2 =

-1.0000 - 1. 4142i
```

If we ask for help about the function equation2 we do the following:

```
>>help equation2
```

This function solves the quadratic equation ax ^ 2 + bx + c = 0
whose coefficients are a, b and c (input parameters)
and whose solutions are x 1 and x 2 (output parameters)

Evaluating a function when its arguments (input parameters) are strings is performed via the command *eval*, whose syntax is as follows:

eval (expression)

This executes the expression when it is a string.

As an example, we evaluate a string that defines a magic square of order 4.

```
>>n=4;
>>eval(['M' num2str(n) ' = magic(n)'])

M4 =

16   2   3  13
 5  11  10   8
 9   7   6  12
 4  14  15   1
```

Local and Global Variables

Typically, each function defined as an M-file contains local variables, i.e., variables that have effect only within the M-file, separate from other M-files and the base workspace. However, it is possible to define variables inside M-files which can take effect simultaneously in other M-files and in the base workspace. For this purpose, it is necessary to define global variables with the GLOBAL command whose syntax is as follows:

GLOBAL x y z...

This defines the variables x, y and z as global.

Any variables defined as global inside a function are available separately for the rest of the functions and in the base workspace command line. If a global variable does not exist, the first time it is used, it will be initialized as an empty array. If there is already a variable with the same name as a global variable being defined, MATLAB will send a warning message and change the value of that variable to match the global variable. It is convenient to declare a variable as global in every function that will need access to it, and also in the command line, in order to access it from the base workspace. The GLOBAL command is located at the beginning of a function (before any occurrence of the variable).

As an example, suppose that we want to study the effect of the interaction coefficients α and β in the Lotka–Volterra predator-prey model:

$$\dot{y}_1 = y_1 - \alpha y_1 y_2$$
$$\dot{y}_2 = -y_2 + \beta y_1 y_2$$

To do this, we create the function *lotka* in the M-file *lotka.m* as depicted in Figure 6-14.

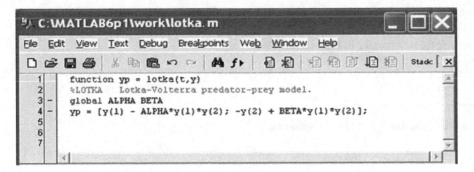

Figure 6-14.

Later, we might type the following in the command line:

```
>>global ALPHA BETA
ALPHA = 0.01
BETA = 0.02
```

These global values may then be used for α and β in the M-file *lotka.m* (without having to specify them). For example, we can generate the graph (Figure 6-15) with the following syntax:

```
>> [t, y] = ode23 ('lotka', 0.10, [1; 1]); plot(t,y)
```

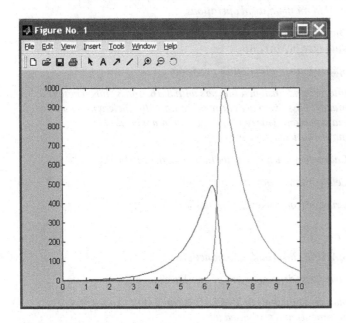

Figure 6-15.

Data Types

MATLAB has 14 different data types, summarized in Figure 6-16 below.

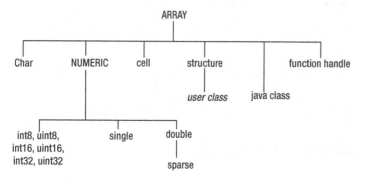

Figure 6-16.

Below are the different types of data:

Data Type	Example	Description
single	3* 10 ^ 38	*Simple numerical precision. This requires less storage than double precision, but it is less precise. This type of data should not be used in mathematical operations.*
Double	3*10^300 5+6i	*Double numerical precision. This is the most commonly used data type in MATLAB.*
sparse	speye(5)	*Sparse matrix with double precision.*
int8, uint8, int16, uint16, int32, uint32	UInt8(magic (3))	*Integers and unsigned integers with 8, 16, and 32 bits. These make it possible to use entire amounts with efficient memory management. This type of data should not be used in mathematical operations.*
char	'Hello'	*Characters (each character has a length of 16 bits).*
cell	{17 'hello' eye (2)}	*Cell (contains data of similar size).*

structure	a.day = 12;
	a.color = 'Red';
	a.mat = magic(3);
		Structure (contains cells of similar size).

user class	inline('sin (x)')	*MATLAB class (built with functions)*
java class	Java.awt.Frame	*Java class (defined in API or own) with Java.*
function handle	@humps	*Manages functions in MATLAB. It can be last in a list of arguments and evaluated with feval.*

Flow Control: FOR Loops, WHILE and IF ELSEIF

The use of recursive functions, conditional operations and piecewise defined functions is very common in mathematics. The handling of loops is necessary for the definition of these types of functions. Naturally, the definition of the functions will be made via *M-files*.

The FOR Loop

MATLAB has its own version of the DO statement (defined in the syntax of most programming languages). This statement allows you to run a command or group of commands repeatedly. For example:

» for i=1:3, x(i)=0, end

X =

0

X =

0   0

X =

0 0 0

The general form of a FOR loop is as follows:

```
for variable = expression
commands
end
```

The loop always starts with the clause *for* and ends with the clause *end*, and includes in its interior a whole set of commands that are separated by commas. If any command defines a variable, it must end with a semicolon in order to avoid repetition in the output. Typically, loops are used in the syntax of M-files. Here is an example (Figure 6-17):

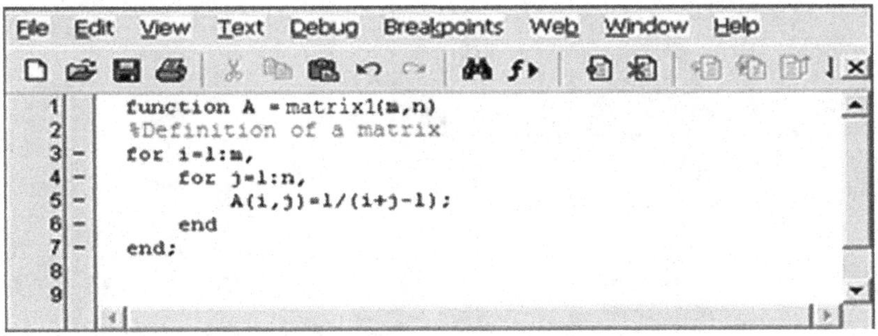

```
function A = matrix1(m,n)
%Definition of a matrix
for i=1:m,
    for j=1:n,
        A(i,j)=1/(i+j-1);
    end
end;
```

Figure 6-17.

In this loop we have defined a Hilbert matrix of order *(m, n)*. If we save it as an M-file *matrix1.m*, we can build any Hilbert matrix later by running the M-file and specifying values for the variables m and n (the matrix dimensions) as shown below:

```
>> M = matrix1 (4,5)
```

M =

1.0000 0.5000 0.3333 0.2500 0.2000
0.5000 0.3333 0.2500 0.2000 0.1667
0.3333 0.2500 0.2000 0.1667 0.1429
0.2500 0.2000 0.1667 0.1429 0.1250

The WHILE Loop

MATLAB has its own version of the WHILE structure defined in the syntax of most programming languages. This statement allows you to repeat a command or group of commands a number of times while a specified logical condition is met. The general syntax of this loop is as follows:

while condition
commands
end

The loop always starts with the clause *while*, followed by a condition, and ends with the clause *end*, and includes in its interior a whole set of commands that are separated by commas which continually loop while the condition is met. If any command defines a variable, it must end with a semicolon in order to avoid repetition in the output. As an example, we write an M-file (Figure 6-18) that is saved as *while1.m*, which calculates the largest number whose factorial does not exceed 10^{100}.

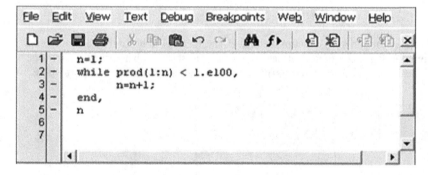

Figure 6-18.

We now run the M-file.

```
>> while1
```

n =

70

IF ELSEIF ELSE END Loops

MATLAB, like most structured programming languages, also includes the IF-ELSEIF-ELSE-END structure. Using this structure, scripts can be run if certain conditions are met. The loop syntax is as follows:

```
if condition
commands
end
```

In this case the commands are executed if the condition is true. But the syntax of this loop may be more general.

```
if condition
commands1
else
commands2
end
```

In this case, the commands *commands1* are executed if the condition is true, and the commands *commands2* are executed if the condition is false.

IF statements and FOR statements can be nested. When multiple IF statements are nested using the ELSEIF statement, the general syntax is as follows:

```
if condition1
commands1
elseif condition2
commands2
elseif condition3
commands3
.
.
else
end
```

In this case, the commands *commands1* are executed if c*ondition1* is true, the commands *commands2* are executed if *condition1* is false and *condition2* is true, the commands *commands3* are executed if *condition1* and *condition2* are false and *condition3* is true, and so on.

The previous nested syntax is equivalent to the following unnested syntax, but executes much faster:

```
if condition1
commands1
else
if condition2
commands2
else
if condition3
commands3
else
.
.
end
end
end
```

Consider, for example, the M-file *else1.m* (see Figure 6-19).

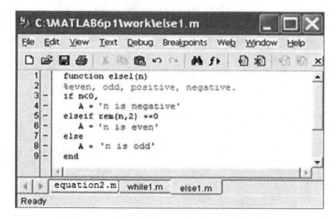

Figure 6-19.

When you run the file it returns negative, odd or even according to whether the argument *n* is negative, non-negative and odd, or non-negative and even, respectively:

>>else1 (8), else1 (5), else1 (- 10)

A =

n is even

A =

n is odd

A =

n is negative

Switch and Case

The *switch* statement executes certain statements based on the value of a variable or expression. Its basic syntax is as follows:

```
switch expression (scalar or string)
casevalue1
statements % runs if expression is value1
casevalue2
statements % runs if expression is value2
.
.
.
otherwise
statements % runs if neither case is satisfied

end
```

Below is an example of a function that returns 'minus one', 'zero', 'one', or 'another value' according to whether the input is equal to −1,0,1 or something else, respectively (Figure 6-20).

```
     function case1(n)
     %-1, 0, 1 or another number.
     switch n
         case -1
             disp('minus one');
         case 0
             disp('zero');
         case 1
             disp('one');
         otherwise
             disp('another value');
     end
```

Figure 6-20.

Running the above example we get:

>> case1 (25)
another value

>> case1 (- 1)
minus one

Continue

The *continue* statement passes control to the next iteration in a *for* loop or *while* loop in which it appears, ignoring the remaining instructions in the body of the loop. Below is an M-file *continue.m* (Figure 6-21) that counts the lines of code in the file *magic.m*, ignoring the white lines and comments.

```
     fid = fopen('magic.m','r');
     count = 0;
     while ~feof(fid)
         line = fgetl(fid);
         if isempty(line) | strncmp(line,'%',1)
             continue
         end
         count = count + 1;
     end
     disp(sprintf('%d lines ',count));
```

Figure 6-21.

Running the M-file, we get:

>> **continue1**
25 lines

Break

The *break* statement terminates the execution of a *for* loop or *while* loop, skipping to the first instruction which appears outside of the loop. Below is an M-file *break1.m* (Figure 6-22) which reads the lines of code in the file *fft.m*, exiting the loop as soon as it encounters the first empty line.

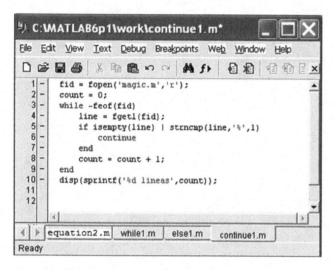

Figure 6-22.

Running the M-file we get:

>> **break1**

```
%FFT Discrete Fourier transform.
%   FFT(X) is the discrete Fourier transform (DFT) of vector X.  For
%   matrices, the FFT operation is applied to each column. For N-D
%   arrays, the FFT operation operates on the first non-singleton
%   dimension.
%
%   FFT(X,N) is the N-point FFT, padded with zeros if X has less
%   than N points and truncated if it has more.
%
%   FFT(X,[],DIM) or FFT(X,N,DIM) applies the FFT operation across the
%   dimension DIM.
%
```

```
%    For length N input vector x, the DFT is a length N vector X,
%    with elements
%                    N
%      X(k) =        sum   x(n)*exp(-j*2*pi*(k-1)*(n-1)/N), 1 <= k <= N.
%                    n=1
%    The inverse DFT (computed by IFFT) is given by
%                    N
%      x(n) = (1/N) sum   X(k)*exp( j*2*pi*(k-1)*(n-1)/N), 1 <= n <= N.
%                    k=1
%
%    See also IFFT, FFT2, IFFT2, FFTSHIFT.
```

Try ... Catch

The instructions between *try* and *catch* are executed until an error occurs. The instruction *lasterr* is used to show the cause of the error. The general syntax of the command is as follows:

```
try,
instruction
...,
instruction
catch,
instruction
...,
instruction
end
```

Return

The *return* statement terminates the current script and returns the control to the invoked function or the keyboard. The following is an example (Figure 6-23) that computes the determinant of a non-empty matrix. If the array is empty it returns the value 1.

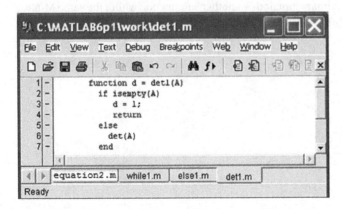

Figure 6-23.

Running the function for a non-empty array we get:

```
>> A = [-1,-1,1; 1,0,1; 1,1,1]

A =
-1 -1 -1
 1  0  1
 1 -1 -1
```

```
>> det1 (A)

ans =

2
```

Now we apply the function to an empty array:

```
>> B =[]

B =

     []
```

```
>> det1 (B)

ans =

     1
```

Subfunctions

M-file-defined functions can contain code for more than one function. The main function in an M-file is called a *primary function*, which is precisely the function which invokes the M-file, but subfunctions hanging from the primary function may be added which are only visible for the primary function or another subfunction within the same M-file. Each subfunction begins with its own function definition. An example is shown in Figure 6-24.

Figure 6-24.

The subfunctions *mean* and *median* calculate the arithmetic mean and the median of the input list. The primary function *newstats* determines the length *n* of the list and calls the subfunctions with the list as the first argument and *n* as the second argument. When executing the main function, it is enough to provide as input a list of values for which the arithmetic mean and median will be calculated. The subfunctions are executed automatically, as shown below.

```
>> [mean, median] = newstats ([10,20,3,4,5,6])
```

mean =

   8

median =

   5.5000

Ordinary Differential Equations Using Numerical Analysis

Obtaining exact solutions of ordinary differential equations is not a simple task. There are a number of different methods for obtaining approximate solutions of ordinary differential equations. These numerical methods include, among others, Euler's method, Heun's method, the Taylor series method, the Runge-Kutta method (implemented in MATLAB's Basic module), the Adams–Bashforth–Moulton method, Milne's method and Hamming's method.

Euler's Method

Suppose we want to solve the differential equation $y' = f(t, y)$, $y(a) = y_0$, on the interval $[a, b]$. We divide the interval $[a, b]$ into M subintervals of the same size using the partition given by the points $t_k = a + kh$, $k = 0,1,\ldots, M$, $h = (b-a)/M$. Euler's method then finds the solution of the differential equation iteratively by calculating $y_{k+1} = y_k + hf(t_k, y_k)$, $k = 0,1, \ldots, M-1$.

Euler's method is implemented using the M-file shown in Figure 6-25.

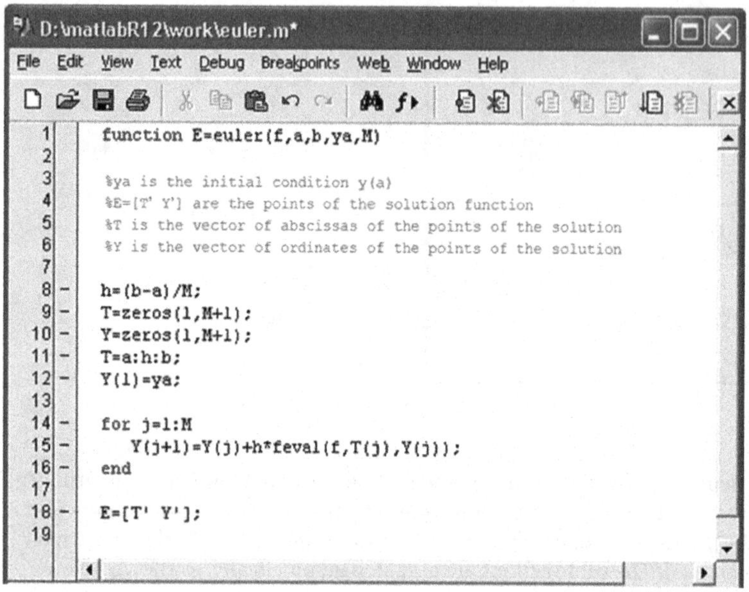
D:\matlabR12\work\euler.m*
File Edit View Text Debug Breakpoints Web Window Help
function E=euler(f,a,b,ya,M)
%ya is the initial condition y(a)
%E=[T' Y'] are the points of the solution function
%T is the vector of abscissas of the points of the solution
%Y is the vector of ordinates of the points of the solution
h=(b-a)/M;
T=zeros(1,M+1);
Y=zeros(1,M+1);
T=a:h:b;
Y(1)=ya;
for j=1:M
Y(j+1)=Y(j)+h*feval(f,T(j),Y(j));
end
E=[T' Y'];

Figure 6-25.

Heun's Method

Suppose we want to solve the differential equation $y' = f(t, y)$, $y(a) = y_0$, on the interval $[a, b]$. We divide the interval $[a, b]$ into M subintervals of the same size using the partition given by the points $t_k = a + kh$, $k = 0,1,\ldots, M$, $h = (b-a)/M$. Heun's method then finds the solution of the differential equation iteratively by calculating $y_{k+1} = y_k + h(f(t_k, y_k) + f(t_{k+1}, y_k + f(t_k, y_k)))/2$, $k = 0,1,\ldots, M-1$.

Heun's method is implemented using the M-file shown in Figure 6-26.

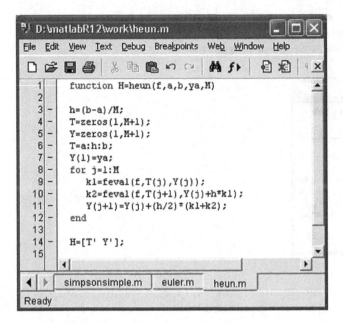

Figure 6-26.

The Taylor Series Method

Suppose we want to solve the differential equation $y' = f(t, y)$, $y(a) = y_0$, on the interval $[a, b]$. We divide the interval $[a, b]$ into M subintervals of the same size using the partition given by the points $t_k = a + kh$, $k = 0, 1, ..., M$, $h = (b-a)/M$. The Taylor series method (let us consider here the method to order 4) finds a solution to the differential equation by evaluating y', y'', y''' and y'''' to give the 4th order Taylor series for y at each partition point.

The Taylor series method is implemented using the M-file shown in Figure 6-27.

```
function T4=taylor(df,a,b,ya,M)

% df=[y' y'' y''' y''''] is the string 'df'
% T4=[T' Y']

h=(b-a)/M;
T=zeros(1,M+1);
Y=zeros(1,M+1);
T=a:h:b;
Y(1)=ya;

for j=1:M
    D=feval(df,T(j),Y(j));
    Y(j+1)=Y(j)+h*(D(1)+h*(D(2)/2+h*(D(3)/6+h*D(4)/24)));
end

T4=[T' Y'];
```

Figure 6-27.

As an example we solve the differential equation $y'(t) = (t - y)/2$ on the interval [0,3], with $y(0) = 1$, using Euler's method, Heun's method and by the Taylor series method.

We will begin by defining the function $f(t, y)$ via the M-file shown in Figure 6-28.

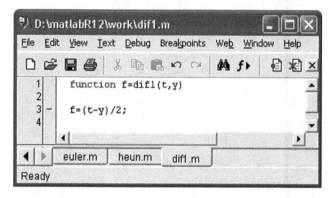

Figure 6-28.

The solution of the equation using Euler's method in 100 steps is calculated as follows:

```
>>E = euler('dif1',0,3,1,100)

E =

0 1.00000000000000
0.03000000000000 0.98500000000000
0.06000000000000 0.97067500000000
0.09000000000000 0.95701487500000
0.12000000000000 0.94400965187500
0.15000000000000 0.93164950709688
0.18000000000000 0.91992476449042
.

.

.
2.85000000000000 1.56377799005910
2.88000000000000 1.58307132020821
2.91000000000000 1.60252525040509
2.94000000000000 1.62213737164901
2.97000000000000 1.64190531107428
3.00000000000000 1.66182673140816
```

This solution can be graphed as follows (see Figure 6-29):

```
>>plot (E (:,2))
```

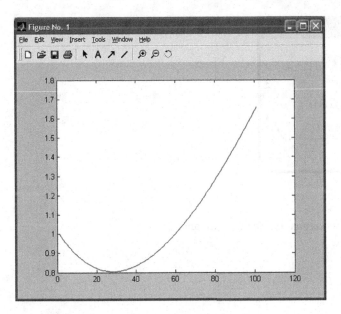

Figure 6-29.

The solution of the equation by Heun's method in 100 steps is calculated as follows:

```
>> H = heun('dif1',0,3,1,100)
H =
0 1.00000000000000
0.03000000000000  0.98533750000000
0.06000000000000  0.97133991296875
0.09000000000000  0.95799734001443
0.12000000000000  0.94530002961496
.
.
.
2.88000000000000  1.59082209379464
2.91000000000000  1.61023972987327
2.94000000000000  1.62981491089478
2.97000000000000  1.64954529140884
3.00000000000000  1.66942856088299
```

The solution using the Taylor series method requires the previously defined function $df = [y' \, y'' \, y''' \, y'''']$ using the M-file shown in Figure 6-30.

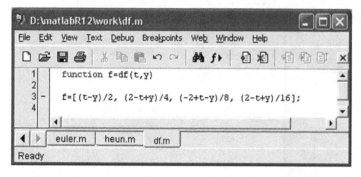

Figure 6-30.

The differential equation is solved by the Taylor series method via the command:

>> T = taylor('df',0,3,1,100)

T =
0 1.00000000000000
0.03000000000000 0.98533581882813
0.06000000000000 0.97133660068283
0.09000000000000 0.95799244555443
0.12000000000000 0.94529360082516
.
.
.
2.88000000000000 1.59078327648360
2.91000000000000 1.61020109213866
2.94000000000000 1.62977645599332
2.97000000000000 1.64950702246046
3.00000000000000 1.66939048087422

EXERCISE 6-1

Find an approximate solution of the following differential equation in the interval [0, 0.8]:

$$y' = t^2 + y^2 \quad y(0) = 1$$

We start by defining the function $f(t,y)$ via the M-file shown in Figure 6-31.

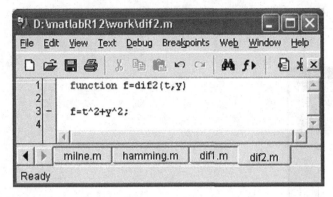

Figure 6-31.

We then solve the differential equation by Euler's method in 20 steps by using the following syntax:

```
>> E = euler('dif2',0,0.8,1,20)
```

E =
```
0 1.00000000000000
0.04000000000000  1.04000000000000
0.08000000000000  1.08332800000000
0.12000000000000  1.13052798222336
0.16000000000000  1.18222772296696
0.20000000000000  1.23915821852503
0.24000000000000  1.30217874214655
0.28000000000000  1.37230952120649
0.32000000000000  1.45077485808625
0.36000000000000  1.53906076564045
0.40000000000000  1.63899308725380
0.44000000000000  1.75284502085643
0.48000000000000  1.88348764754208
0.52000000000000  2.03460467627982
0.56000000000000  2.21100532382941
0.60000000000000  2.41909110550949
0.64000000000000  2.66757117657970
0.68000000000000  2.96859261586445
0.72000000000000  3.33959030062305
0.76000000000000  3.80644083566367
0.80000000000000  4.40910450907999
```

The solution can be graphed (Figure 6-32) as follows:

```
>> plot(E(:,2))
```

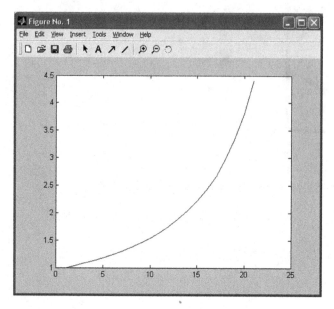

Figure 6-32.

■ ■ ■

CHAPTER 7

Ordinary and Partial Differential Equations with Initial and Boundary Values

Numerical Solutions of Differential Equations

MATLAB provides commands in its Basic module allowing for the numerical solution of ordinary differential equations (ODEs), differential algebraic equations (DAEs) and boundary value problems. It is also possible to solve systems of differential equations with boundary values and parabolic and elliptic partial differential equations.

Ordinary Differential Equations with Initial Values

An ordinary differential equation contains one or more derivatives of the dependent variable y with respect to the independent variable t. A first order ordinary differential equation with an initial value for the independent variable can be represented as:

$$y' = f(t,y)$$
$$y(t_0) = y_0$$

The previous problem can be generalized to the case where y is a vector, $y = (y_1, y_2, ..., y_n)$.

MATLAB's Basic module commands relating to ordinary differential equations and differential algebraic equations with initial values are presented in the following table:

Command	Class of Problem Solving, Numerical Method and Syntax
ode45	*Ordinary differential equations by the Runge–Kutta method*
ode23	*Ordinary differential equations by the Runge–Kutta method*
ode113	*Ordinary differential equations by Adams' method*
ode15s	*Differential algebraic equations and ordinary differential equations using NDFs (BDFs)*
ode23s	*Ordinary differential equations by the Rosenbrock method*
ode23t	*Ordinary differential and differential algebraic equations by the trapezoidal rule*
ode23tb	*Ordinary differential equations using TR-BDF2*

The common syntax for the previous seven commands is the following:

```
[T, y] = solver(odefun,tspan,y0)
[T, y] = solver(odefun,tspan,y0,options)
[T, y] = solver(odefun,tspan,y0,options,p1,p2...)
[T, y, TE, YE, IE] = solver(odefun,tspan,y0,options)
```

In the above, *solver* can be any of the commands *ode45, ode23, ode113, ode15s, ode23s, ode23t,* or *ode23tb*.

The argument odefun evaluates the right-hand side of the differential equation or system written in the form $y' = f(t, y)$ or $M(t, y)y' = f(t, y)$, where $M(t, y)$ is called a mass matrix. The command *ode23s* can only solve equations with constant mass matrix. The commands *ode15s* and *ode23t* can solve algebraic differential equations and systems of ordinary differential equations with a singular mass matrix. The argument tspan is a vector that specifies the range of integration $[t_0, t_f]$ (*tspan*= $[t_0, t_1,...,t_f]$, which must be either an increasing or decreasing list, is used to obtain solutions for specific values of t).The argument y_0 specifies a vector of initial conditions. The arguments *p1, p2,...* are optional parameters that are passed to *odefun*. The argument *options* specifies additional integration options using the command options *odeset* which can be found in the program manual. The vectors T and y present the numerical values of the independent and dependent variables for the solutions found.

As a first example we find solutions in the interval [0,12] of the following system of ordinary differential equations:

$$\begin{aligned} y_1' &= y_2 y_3 & y_1(0) &= 0 \\ y_2' &= -y_1 y_3 & y_2(0) &= 1 \\ y_3' &= -0.51 y_1 y_2 & y_3(0) &= 1 \end{aligned}$$

For this, we define a function named *system1* in an M-file, which will store the equations of the system. The function begins by defining a column vector with three rows which are subsequently assigned components that make up the syntax of the three equations (Figure 7-1).

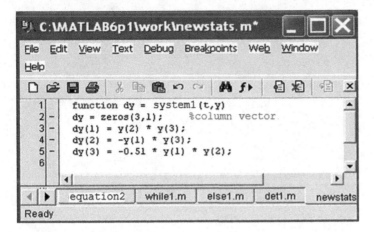

Figure 7-1.

We then solve the system by typing the following in the Command Window:

```
>> [T, Y] = ode45(@system1,[0 12],[0 1 1])
```

T =

0
0.0001
0.0001
0.0002
0.0002
0.0005
.
.
11.6136
11.7424
11.8712
12.0000

Y =

0 1.0000 1.0000
0.0001 1.0000 1.0000
0.0001 1.0000 1.0000
0.0002 1.0000 1.0000
0.0002 1.0000 1.0000
0.0005 1.0000 1.0000
0.0007 1.0000 1.0000
0.0010 1.0000 1.0000
0.0012 1.0000 1.0000
0.0025 1.0000 1.0000
0.0037 1.0000 1.0000
0.0050 1.0000 1.0000
0.0062 1.0000 1.0000

```
0.0125  0.9999  1.0000
0.0188  0.9998  0.9999
0.0251  0.9997  0.9998
0.0313  0.9995  0.9997
0.0627  0.9980  0.9990
 .
 .
 0.8594-0.5105  0.7894
 0.7257-0.6876  0.8552
 0.5228-0.8524  0.9281
 0.2695-0.9631  0.9815
-0.0118-0.9990  0.9992
-0.2936-0.9540  0.9763
-0.4098-0.9102  0.9548
-0.5169-0.8539  0.9279
-0.6135-0.7874  0.8974
-0.6987-0.7128  0.8650
```

To better interpret the results, the above numerical solution can be graphed (Figure 7-2) by using the following command:

```
>> plot (T, Y(:,1), '-', T, Y(:,2),'-', T, Y(:,3),'. ')
```

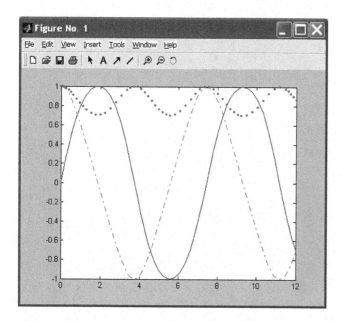

Figure 7-2.

Ordinary Differential Equations with Boundary Values

MATLAB also allows you to solve ordinary differential equations with boundary conditions. The boundary conditions specify a relationship that must hold between the values of the solution function at the end points of the interval on which it is defined. The simplest problem of this type is the system of equations

$$y' = f(x, y)$$

where x is the independent variable, y is the dependent variable and y' is the derivative *with respect to x* (i.e., $y' = dy/dx$). In addition, the solution on the interval $[a, b]$ has to meet the following boundary condition:

$$g(y(a), y(b)) = 0$$

More generally this type of differential equation can be expressed as follows:

$$y' = f(x, y, p)$$
$$g(y(a), y(b), p) = 0$$

where the vector p consists of parameters which have to be determined simultaneously with the solution via the boundary conditions.

The command that solves these problems is *bvp4c*, whose syntax is as follows:

```
Sol = bvp4c (odefun, bcfun, solinit)
Sol = bvp4c (odefun, bcfun, solinit, options)
Sol = bvp4c (odefun, bcfun, solinit, options, p1, p2...)
```

In the syntax above *odefun* is a function that evaluates $f(x, y)$. It may take one of the following forms:

```
dydx = odefun(x, y)
dydx = odefun(x, y, p1, p2, ...)
dydx = odefun(x, y, parameters)
dydx = odefun(x, y, parameters, p1, p2, ...)
```

The argument *bcfun* in *bvp4c* is a function that computes the residual in the boundary conditions. Its form is as follows:

```
Res = bcfun(ya, yb)
Res = bcfun(ya, yb, p1, p2, ...)
Res = bcfun(ya, yb, parameters)
Res = bcfun(ya, yb, parameters, p1, p2, ...)
```

The argument *solinit* is a structure containing an initial guess of the solution. It has the following fields: x (which gives the ordered nodes of the initial mesh so that the boundary conditions are imposed at $a = $ solinit.x(1) and $b = $ solinit.x(end)); and y (the initial guess for the solution, given as a vector, so that the i-th entry is a constant guess for the i-th component of the solution at all the mesh points given by x). The structure *solinit* is created using the command *bvpinit*. The syntax is solinit = bvpinit(x,y).

As an example we solve the second order differential equation:

$$y'' + |y| = 0$$

whose solutions must satisfy the boundary conditions:

$$y_1(0) = 0$$
$$y(4) = -2$$

This is equivalent to the following problem (where $y_1 = y$ and $y_2 = y'$):

$$y_1' = y_2$$
$$y_2' = -|y_1|$$

We consider a mesh of five equally spaced points in the interval [0,4] and our initial guess for the solution is $y_1 = 1$ and $y_2 = 0$. These assumptions are included in the following syntax:

>> **solinit = bvpinit (linspace (0,4,5), [1 0]);**

The M-files depicted in Figures 7-3 and 7-4 show how to enter the equation and its boundary conditions.

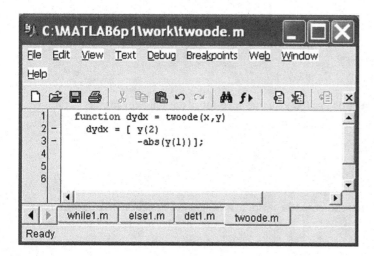

Figure 7-3.

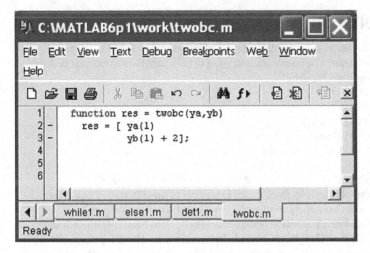

```
function res = twobc(ya,yb)
  res = [ ya(1)
          yb(1) + 2];
```

Figure 7-4.

The following syntax is used to find the solution of the equation:

```
>> Sun = bvp4c (@twoode, @twobc, solinit);
```

The solution can be graphed (Figure 7-5) using the command *bvpval* as follows:

```
>> y = bvpval (Sun, linspace (0,4));
>> plot (x, y(1,:));
```

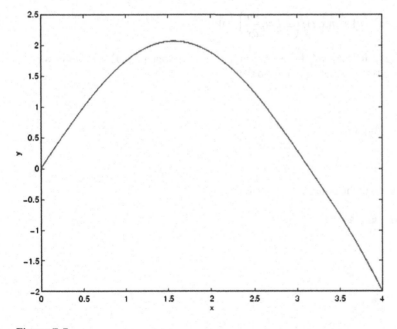

Figure 7-5.

Partial Differential Equations

MATLAB's Basic module has features that enable you to solve partial differential equations and systems of partial differential equations with initial boundary conditions. The basic function used to calculate the solutions is *pedepe*, and the basic function used to evaluate these solutions is *pdeval*.

The syntax of the function *pedepe* is as follows:

```
Sol = pdepe (m, pdefun, icfun, bcfun, xmesh, tspan)
Sol = pdepe (m, pdefun, icfun, bcfun, xmesh, tspan, options)
Sun = pdepe(m, pdefun, icfun, bcfun, xmesh, tspan, options, p1, p2...)
```

The parameter *m* takes the value 0, 1 or 2 according to the nature of the symmetry of the problem (block, cylindrical or spherical, respectively). The argument *pdefun* defines the components of the differential equation, *icfun* defines the initial conditions, *bcfun* defines the boundary conditions, *xmesh* and *tspan* are vectors $[x_0, x_1,...,x_n]$ and $[t_0, t_1,...,t_f]$ that specify the points at which a numerical solution is requested $(n, f \geq 3)$, *options* specifies some calculation options of the underlying solver (RelTol, AbsTol, NormControl, InitialStep and MaxStep to specify relative tolerance, absolute tolerance, norm tolerance, initial step and max step, respectively) and *p1, p2,...* are parameters to pass to the functions *pdefun, icfun* and *bcfun*.

pdepe solves partial differential equations of the form:

$$c\left(x,t,u,\frac{\partial u}{\partial x}\right)\frac{\partial u}{\partial t} = x^{-m}\frac{\partial}{\partial x}\left(x^m f\left(x,t,u,\frac{\partial u}{\partial x}\right)\right) + s\left(x,t,u,\frac{\partial u}{\partial x}\right)$$

where $a \leq x \leq b$ and $t_0 \leq t \leq t_f$. Moreover, for $t = t_0$ and for all x the solution components meet the initial conditions:

$$u(x,t_0) = u_0(x)$$

and for all *t* and each $x = a$ or $x = b$, the solution components satisfy the boundary conditions of the form:

$$p(x,t,u) + q(x,t)f\left(x,t,u,\frac{\partial u}{\partial x}\right) = 0$$

In addition, we have that *a*= xmesh (1), b = xmesh (end), tspan (1) =t_0 and tspan (end) = t_f. Moreover *pdefun* finds the terms *c, f* and *s* of the partial differential equation, so that:

```
[c, f, s] = pdefun (x, t, u, dudx)
```

Similiarly *icfun* evaluates the initial conditions

```
u = icfun (x)
```

Finally, *bcfun* evaluates the terms *p* and *q* of the boundary conditions:

```
[pl, ql, pr, qr] = bcfun (xl, ul, xr, ur, t)
```

As a first example we solve the following partial differential equation ($x \in [0,1]$ and $t \geq 0$):

$$\pi^2 \frac{\partial u}{\partial t} = \frac{\partial}{\partial x}\left(\frac{\partial u}{\partial x}\right)$$

satisfying the initial condition:

$$u(x, 0) = \sin \pi x$$

and the boundary conditions:

$$u(0, t) \equiv 0$$

$$\pi e^{-t} + \frac{\partial u}{\partial x}(1, t) = 0$$

We begin by defining functions in M-files as shown in Figures 7-6 to 7-8.

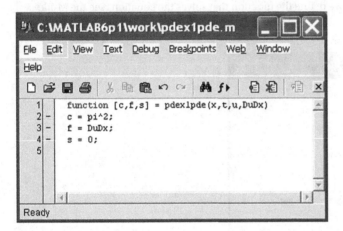

Figure 7-6.

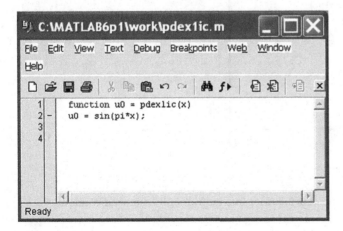

Figure 7-7.

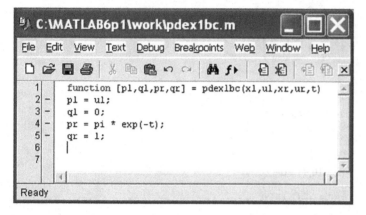

```
C:\MATLAB6p1\work\pdex1bc.m

File  Edit  View  Text  Debug  Breakpoints  Web  Window  Help

1      function [pl,ql,pr,qr] = pdex1bc(xl,ul,xr,ur,t)
2  -    pl = ul;
3  -    ql = 0;
4  -    pr = pi * exp(-t);
5  -    qr = 1;
6
7

Ready
```

Figure 7-8.

Once the support functions have been defined, we define the function that solves the equation (see the M-file in Figure 7-9).

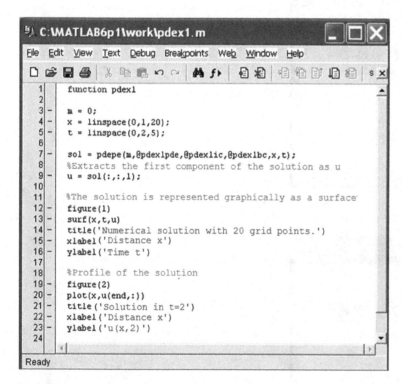

```
C:\MATLAB6p1\work\pdex1.m

File  Edit  View  Text  Debug  Breakpoints  Web  Window  Help

1      function pdex1
2
3  -    m = 0;
4  -    x = linspace(0,1,20);
5  -    t = linspace(0,2,5);
6
7  -    sol = pdepe(m,@pdex1pde,@pdex1ic,@pdex1bc,x,t);
8      %Extracts the first component of the solution as u
9  -    u = sol(:,:,1);
10
11     %The solution is represented graphically as a surface
12 -    figure(1)
13 -    surf(x,t,u)
14 -    title('Numerical solution with 20 grid points.')
15 -    xlabel('Distance x')
16 -    ylabel('Time t')
17
18     %Profile of the solution
19 -    figure(2)
20 -    plot(x,u(end,:))
21 -    title('Solution in t=2')
22 -    xlabel('Distance x')
23 -    ylabel('u(x,2)')
24

Ready
```

Figure 7-9.

To view the solution (Figures 7-10 and 7-11), we enter the following into the MATLAB Command Window:

>> pdex1

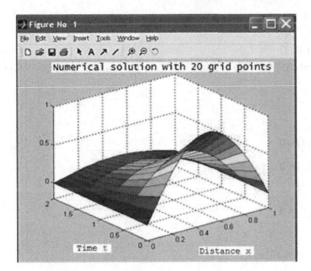

Figure 7-10.

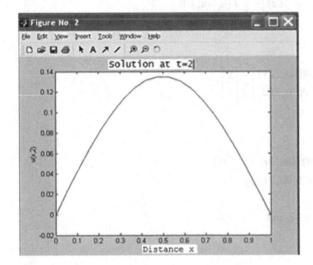

Figure 7-11.

As a second example we solve the following system of partial differential equations ($x \in [0,1]$ and $t \geq 0$):

$$\frac{\partial u_1}{\partial t} = 0.024\frac{\partial^2 u_1}{\partial x^2} - F(u_1 - u_2)$$

$$\frac{\partial u_2}{\partial t} = 0.170\frac{\partial^2 u_2}{\partial x^2} + F(u_1 - u_2)$$

$$F(y) = \exp(5.73y) - \exp(-11.46y)$$

111

satisfying the initial conditions:

$$u_1(x, 0) \equiv 1$$
$$u_2(x, 0) \equiv 0$$

and the boundary conditions:

$$\frac{\partial u_1}{\partial x}(0, t) \equiv 0$$
$$u_2(0, t) \equiv 0$$
$$u_1(1, t) \equiv 1$$
$$\frac{\partial u_2}{\partial x}(1, t) \equiv 0$$

To conveniently use the function *pdepe*, the system can be written as:

$$\begin{bmatrix} 1 \\ 1 \end{bmatrix} .* \frac{\partial}{\partial t}\begin{bmatrix} u_1 \\ u_2 \end{bmatrix} = \frac{\partial}{\partial x}\begin{bmatrix} 0.024(\partial u_1 / \partial x) \\ 0.170(\partial u_2 / \partial x) \end{bmatrix} + \begin{bmatrix} -F(u_1 - u_2) \\ F(u_1 - u_2) \end{bmatrix}$$

The left boundary condition can be written as:

$$\begin{bmatrix} 0 \\ u_2 \end{bmatrix} + \begin{bmatrix} 1 \\ 0 \end{bmatrix} .* \begin{bmatrix} 0.024(\partial u_1 / \partial x) \\ 0.170(\partial u_2 / \partial x) \end{bmatrix} = \begin{bmatrix} 0 \\ 0 \end{bmatrix}$$

and the right boundary condition can be written as:

$$\begin{bmatrix} u_1 - 1 \\ 0 \end{bmatrix} + \begin{bmatrix} 0 \\ 1 \end{bmatrix} .* \begin{bmatrix} 0.024(\partial u_1 / \partial x) \\ 0.170(\partial u_2 / \partial x) \end{bmatrix} = \begin{bmatrix} 0 \\ 0 \end{bmatrix}$$

We start by defining the functions in M-files as shown in Figures 7-12 to 7-14.

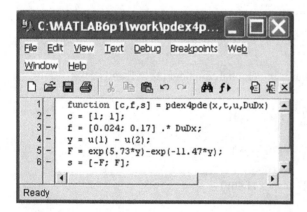

Figure 7-12.

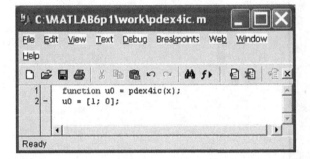

```
C:\MATLAB6p1\work\pdex4bc.m
File  Edit  View  Text  Debug  Breakpoints  Web  Window  Help

1       function [pl,ql,pr,qr] = pdex4bc(xl,ul,xr,ur,t)
2  -    pl = [0; ul(2)];
3  -    ql = [1; 0];
4  -    pr = [ur(1)-1; 0];
5  -    qr = [0; 1];

Ready
```

Figure 7-13.

```
C:\MATLAB6p1\work\pdex4ic.m
File  Edit  View  Text  Debug  Breakpoints  Web  Window
Help

1       function u0 = pdex4ic(x);
2  -    u0 = [1; 0];

Ready
```

Figure 7-14.

Once the support functions are defined, the function that solves the system of equations is given by the M-file shown in Figure 7-15.

```
C:\MATLAB6p1\work\pdex4.m
File  Edit  View  Text  Debug  Breakpoints  Web  Window  Help                          Stad

1       function pdex4
2  -    m = 0;
3  -    x = [0 0.005 0.01 0.05 0.1 0.2 0.5 0.7 0.9 0.95 0.99 0.995 1];
4  -    t = [0 0.005 0.01 0.05 0.1 0.5 1 1.5 2];
5
6  -    sol = pdepe(m,@pdex4pde,@pdex4ic,@pdex4bc,x,t);
7  -    ul = sol(:,:,1);
8  -    u2 = sol(:,:,2);
9
10 -    figure
11 -    surf(x,t,ul)
12 -    title('ul(x,t)')
13 -    xlabel('Distance x')
14 -    ylabel('Time t')
15
16 -    figure
17 -    surf(x,t,u2)
18 -    title('u2(x,t)')
19 -    xlabel('Distance x')
20 -    ylabel ('Time t')
21

Ready
```

Figure 7-15.

To view the solution (Figures 7-16 and 7-17), we enter the following in the MATLAB Command Window:

>> pdex4

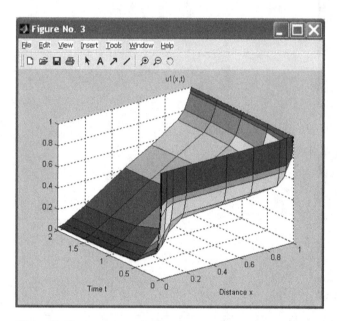

Figure 7-16.

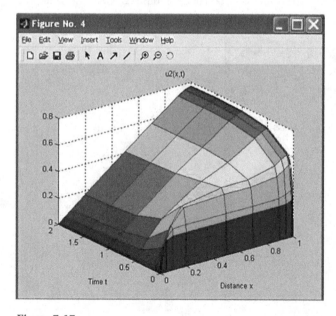

Figure 7-17.

EXERCISE 7-1

Solve the following Van der Pol system of equations:

$$y_1' = y_2 \qquad\qquad y_1(0) = 0$$
$$y_2' = 1000(1 - y_1^2)y_2 - y_1 \quad y_2(0) = 1$$

We begin by defining a function named *vdp100* in an M-file, where we will store the equations of the system. This function begins by defining a vector column with two empty rows which are subsequently assigned the components which make up the equation (Figure 7-18).

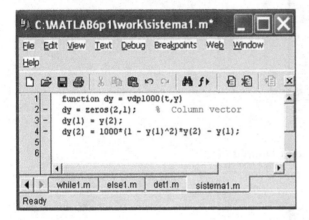

Figure 7-18.

We then solve the system and plot the solution $y_1 = y_1(t)$ given by the first column (Figure 7-19) by typing the following into the Command Window:

```
>> [T, Y] = ode15s(@vdp1000,[0 3000],[2 0]);
>> plot (T, Y(:,1),'-')
```

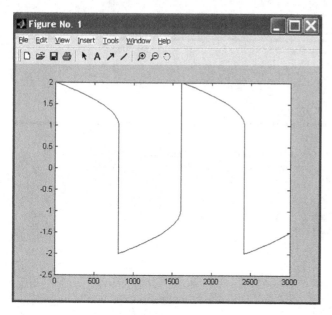

Figure 7-19.

Similarly we plot the solution $y_2 = y_2(t)$ (Figure 7-20) by using the syntax:

```
>> plot (T, Y(:,2),'-')
```

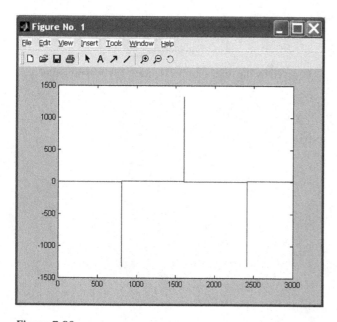

Figure 7-20.

EXERCISE 7-2

Given the following differential equation

$$y'' + (\lambda - 2q\cos(2x))y = 0$$

subject to the boundary conditions $y(0) = 1$, $y'(0) = 0$, $y'(\pi) = 0$, find a solution for $q = 5$ and $\lambda = 15$ based on an initial solution defined on 10 equally spaced points in the interval $[0, \pi]$ and graph the first component of the solution on 100 equally spaced points in the interval $[0, \pi]$.

The given equation is equivalent to the following system of first order differential equations:

$$y_1' = y_2$$
$$y_2' = -(\lambda - 2q\cos 2x))$$

with the following boundary conditions:

$$y_1(0) - 1 = 0$$
$$y_2(0) = 0$$
$$y_2(\pi) = 0$$

The system of equations is introduced in the M-file shown in Figure 7-21, the boundary conditions are given in the M-file shown in Figure 7-22, and the M-file in Figure 7-23 sets up the initial solution.

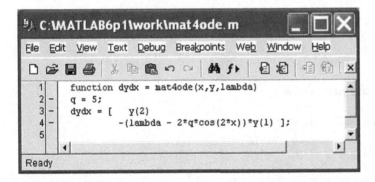

```
function dydx = mat4ode(x,y,lambda)
q = 5;
dydx = [    y(2)
            -(lambda - 2*q*cos(2*x))*y(1) ];
```

Figure 7-21.

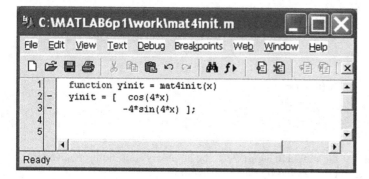

```
⚙ C:\MATLAB6p1\work\mat4bc.m            _ □ X

File  Edit  View  Text  Debug  Breakpoints  Web  Window  Help

 □ ☞ ▤ ⚙   ✂ ▤ ▤ ↺ ↻   ▲ ƒ▸   ▤ ▨   ▥ ▥  ×

 1      function res = mat4bc(ya,yb,lambda)
 2 -    res = [   ya(2)
 3 -              yb(2)
 4 -              ya(1)-1 ];
 5

 ◀                                      ▶

Ready
```

Figure 7-22.

```
⚙ C:\MATLAB6p1\work\mat4init.m          _ □ X

File  Edit  View  Text  Debug  Breakpoints  Web  Window  Help

 □ ☞ ▤ ⚙   ✂ ▤ ▤ ↺ ↻   ▲ ƒ▸   ▤ ▨   ▥ ▥  ×

 1      function yinit = mat4init(x)
 2 -    yinit = [   cos(4*x)
 3 -                -4*sin(4*x) ];
 4
 5

 ◀                                      ▶

Ready
```

Figure 7-23.

The initial solution for $\lambda = 15$ and 10 equally spaced points in $[0, \pi]$ is calculated using the following MATLAB syntax:

```
>> lambda = 15;
solinit = bvpinit (linspace(0,pi,10), @mat4init, lambda);
```

The numerical solution of the system is calculated using the following syntax:

```
>> sol = bvp4c(@mat4ode,@mat4bc,solinit);
```

To graph the first component on 100 equally spaced points in the interval $[0, \pi]$ we use the following syntax:

```
>> xint = linspace(0,pi);
Sxint = bvpval (ground, xint);
plot (xint, Sxint(1,:)))
axis([0 pi-1 1.1])
xlabel ('x')
ylabel('solution y')
```

The result is shown in Figure 7-24.

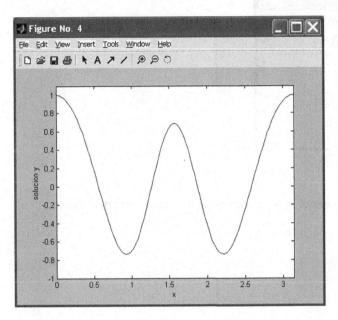

Figure 7-24.

EXERCISE 7-3

Solve the following differential equation

$$y'' + (1 - y^2)y' + y = 0$$

in the interval [0,20], taking as initial solution $y = 2$, $y' = 0$. Solve the more general equation

$$y'' + \mu(1 - y^2)y' + y = 0 \quad \mu > 0.$$

The general equation above is equivalent to the following system of first-order linear equations:

$$y_1' - = y_2$$
$$y_2' - = \mu(1 - y_1^2)y_2 - y_1$$

which is defined for $\mu = 1$ in the M-file shown in Figure 7-25.

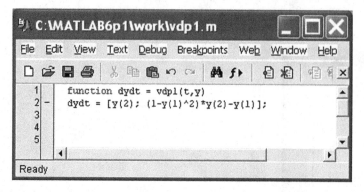

Figure 7-25.

Taking the initial solution $y_1 = 2$ and $y_2 = 0$ in the interval $[0, 20]$, we can solve the system using the following MATLAB syntax:

```
>> [t, y] = ode45(@vdp1,[0 20],[2; 0])

t =

0
0.0000
0.0001
0.0001
0.0001
0.0002
0.0004
0.0005
0.0006
0.0012
.
.
19.9559
19.9780
20,0000

y =

2.0000 0
2.0000 - 0.0001
2.0000 - 0.0001
2.0000 - 0.0002
2.0000 - 0.0002
2.0000 - 0.0005
.
.
```

1.8729 1.0366
1.9358 0.7357
1.9787 0.4746
2.0046 0.2562
2.0096 0.1969
2.0133 0.1413
2.0158 0.0892
2.0172 0.0404

We can graph the solutions using the following syntax (see Figure 7-26):

```
>> plot (t, y(:,1),'-', t, y(:,2),'-')
>> xlabel ('time t')
>> ylabel('solution y')
>> legend ('y_1', 'y_2')
```

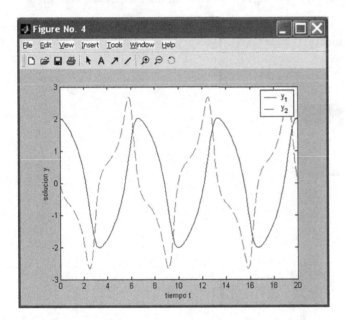

Figure 7-26.

To solve the general system with the parameter μ, we define the system in the M-file shown in Figure 7-27.

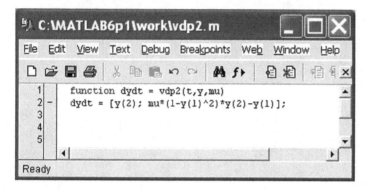

Figure 7-27.

Now we can graph the first solution $y_1 = 2$ and $y_2 = 0$ corresponding to $\mu = 1000$ in the interval $[0,1500]$ using the following syntax (see Figure 7-28):

```
>> [t, y] = ode15s(@vdp2,[0 1500],[2; 0],[],1000);
>> xlabel ('time t')
>> ylabel ('solution y_1')
```

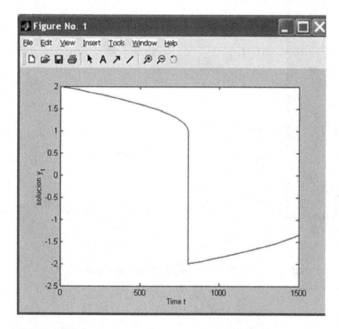

Figure 7-28.

To graph the first solution $y_1 = 2$ and $y_2 = 0$ for another value of the parameter, for example $\mu = 100$, in the interval [0,1500], we use the following syntax (see Figure 7-29):

```
>> [t, y] = ode15s(@vdp2,[0 1500],[2; 0],[],100);
>> plot (t, y(:,1),'-');
```

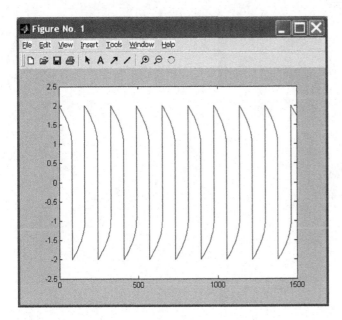

Figure 7-29.

CHAPTER 8

■ ■ ■

Symbolic Differential and Integral Calculus

Symbolic Computation with MATLAB. Symbolic Variables

MATLAB's *Symbolic Math Toolbox* module allows you to easily manipulate and operate on formulae and expressions symbolically. It is possible to expand, factor and simplify polynomials and rational and trigonometric expressions; find algebraic solutions of polynomial equations and systems of equations; evaluate derivatives and integrals symbolically; find symbolic solutions of differential equations; manipulate powers, limits and many other facets of algebraic series. To do this, MATLAB first requires that all variables (or algebraic expressions) are declared as symbolic with the command *syms* (or *sym*). For example, if we want to treat $6*a*b + 3*a^2 + 2*a*b$ as a symbolic expression and simplify it, we first need to declare the two variables a and b as symbolic as follows:

```
>> syms a b
>> simplify(6*a*b + 3*a^2 + 2*a*b)
```

ans =
$8 * a * b + 3 * a ^ 2$

Alternatively, we could have used the following expression:

```
>> simplify(sym('6*a*b + 3*a^2 + 2*a*b'))
```

ans =

$8 * a * b + 3 * a ^2$

The MATLAB *symbolic mathtoolbox* provides several commands which can be used to define and manipulate symbolic variables. These are described below:

syms x y z... t	*Creates symbolic variables x, y, z,..., t.*
syms x y z... t real	*Creates symbolic variables x, y, z,..., t and assumes they are real.*
syms x y z... t unreal	*Creates symbolic variables x, y, z,..., t and assumes that they are not real.*
syms	*Lists the symbolic variables in the workspace.*
x = sym ('x')	*The variable x becomes symbolic (equivalent to syms x).*
x = sym ('x', real)	*The variable x becomes a real symbolic variable.*
x = sym('x',unreal)	*The variable x becomes a non-real symbolic variable.*
s = sym (A)	*Creates a symbolic object from A, where A may be a string, a scalar, an array, a numeric expression, etc.*
s = sym (A, 'option')	*Converts an array, scalar or numeric expression A to a symbolic object according to the specified option. The option can be 'f' for floating point, 'r' for rational, 'e' for an error format or 'd' for decimal.*
double(x)	*Converts the variable or expression x to numeric double-precision.*
sym2poly (poly)	*Returns a vector whose components are the coefficients the symbolic polynomial poly.*
poly2sym (vector)	*Returns a symbolic polynomial whose coefficients are the components of the vector vector.*
poly2sym(vector, 'v')	*Returns a symbolic polynomial in the variable v whose coefficients are the components of the vector vector.*
char (X)	*Converts the array X of non-negative integers (interpreted as ASCII values) into a character string.*
latex (S)	*Convers the symbolic expression S into Latex code.*
ccode (S)	*Converts a symbolic expression S into C code.*
fortran (s)	*Converts a symbolic expression S into Fortran code.*
pretty (expr)	*Converts a symbolic expression into typeset mathematics.*
digits (d)	*Returns symbolic variables with a precision of d significant decimal digits.*
digits	*Returns the current accuracy for symbolic variables.*
vpa (expr)	*Returns the numerical result of the expression to the number of significant digits specified by digits.*
vpa (expr, n)	*Returns the numerical result of the expression to n significant decimal digits.*
vpa('expr', n)	*Numerical result of the expression to n significant decimal digits.*
findsym (S)	*Returns all the symbolic variables in the symbolic expression or symbolic matrix S.*
isvarname (S)	*Returns TRUE if S is a valid symbolic variable.*
vectorize (S)	*Inserts a point in the string S before any symbol ^, * or / .*

As a first example we consider $H = 3a^2 - 2a + 7$, $F = 6a^3 - 5a + 2$ and $G = 5a^2 + 4a - 3$, and calculate: $H + F + G$, $H - F + G$ and $H - F - G$.

```
>> syms a
>> H = 3*a^2 - 2*a + 7; F = 6*a^3 - 5*a + 2; G = 5*a^2 + 4*a - 3;
>> pretty(H+F+G)
```

```
    2           3
8 a  - 3 a + 6 + 6 a
```

```
>> pretty(H-F+G)
```

```
    2           3
8 a  + 7 a + 2 - 6 a
```

```
>> pretty(H-F-G)
```

```
     2          3
-2 a  - a + 8 - 6 a
```

In the following example, we carry out the following symbolic rational operations:

$$\frac{1}{2a} + \frac{1}{3b} + \frac{1}{4a} + \frac{1}{5b} + \frac{1}{6c}, \frac{1-a^9}{1-a^3} \text{ and } \frac{1}{1+a} + \frac{1}{(1+a)^2} + \frac{1}{(1+a)^3}.$$

We will begin by defining the variables a, b and c as symbolic and subsequently perform the specified operations.

```
>> syms a b c
>> pretty(1/(2*a)+1/(3*b)+1/(4*a)+1/(5*b)+1/(6*c))
```

```
3/4 1/a + 8/15 1/b + 1/6 1/c
```

```
>> pretty((1-a)^9/(1-a)^3)
```

```
      6
(1 - a)
```

```
>> pretty(1/(1+a)+1/(1+a)^2+1/(1+a)^3)
```

```
  1         1          1
----- + -------- + --------
1 + a        2          3
        (1 + a)    (1 + a)
```

```
>> pretty (simplify (1 /(1+a) + 1 /(1+a) ^ 2 + 1 /(1+a) ^ 3))
```

```
         2
3 + 3 a + a
------------
         3
(1 + a)
```

127

Next we calculate $\sqrt{2}+3\sqrt{2}-\dfrac{\sqrt{2}}{2}$ and $\dfrac{1}{1+\sqrt{2}}+\dfrac{1}{1-\sqrt{2}}$ symbolically.

```
>> pretty(sym(sqrt(2)+3*sqrt(2)-sqrt(2)/2))
```

```
        1/2
7/2 2
```

```
>> pretty (sym (1 / (1 + sqrt (2)) + 1 / (1-sqrt (2))))
```

```
-2
```

In the following example, we calculate $\dfrac{1}{2+\sqrt{5}}$ symbolically and pass the result to numerical form.

```
>> r=sym(1/(2+sqrt(5)))
```

```
r =
```

```
8505245244017276*2^(-55)
```

```
>> numeric(r)
```

```
ans =
0.24
```

We then solve the equation $x^4+1=0$ and present the result in typeset mathematical form.

```
>> solve('x^4+1=0')
```

```
ans =
```

```
[   1/2*2^(1/2)+1/2*i*2^(1/2)]
[  -1/2*2^(1/2)-1/2*i*2^(1/2)]
[   1/2*2^(1/2)-1/2*i*2^(1/2)]
[  -1/2*2^(1/2)+1/2*i*2^(1/2)]
```

```
>> pretty(solve('x^4+1=0'))
```

```
[        1/2          1/2 ]
[1/2/2 + 1/2 i 2]
[                        ]
[        1/2          1/2]
[-1/2 2 - 1/2 i 2]
[                        ]
[        1/2          1/2 ]
[1/2 2 - 1/2 i 2]
[                        ]
[        1/2          1/2]
[-1/2 2 + 1/2 i 2]
```

Next we transform a vector to a polynomial and vice versa.

```
>> pretty(poly2sym([1 0 9 6 2]))
```

```
 4      2
x  + 9 x  + 6 x + 2
```

```
>> sym2poly(x^4+9*x^2+6*x+2)
```

ans =

```
1.00 0 9.00 6.00 2.00
```

Below is a Hilbert matrix of order 2 whose entries have been evaluated to five significant decimal digits.

```
>> vpa (hilb (2), 5)
```

ans =

```
[1.,. 50000]
[. 50000,. 33333]
```

In the following example we define a symbolic matrix and calculate its determinant.

```
>> syms x
A = [cos(a*x), sin(a*x);-sin(a*x), cos(a*x)]
```

A =

```
[cos(a*x), sin(a*x)]
[-sin(a*x), cos(a*x)]
```

```
>> det (A)
```

ans =

```
cos(a*x) ^ 2 + sin(a*x) ^ 2
```

Next we define the previous symbolic matrix in an alternative form and calculate its inverse.

```
>> A = sym ([cos(a*x), sin(a*x);-sin(a*x), cos(a*x)])
```

A =

```
[cos(a*x), sin(a*x)]
[-sin(a*x), cos(a*x)]
```

>> *pretty (inv (A))*

```
                [cos(a x)        sin(a x)]
                [--------    -  --------]
                [   %1            %1    ]
                [                        ]
                [sin(a x)        cos (a x)]
                [--------        -------- ]
                [   %1            %1     ]

                     2            2
            %1: = cos(a x) + sin(a x)
```

In the following example, we calculate $1/2 + 1/3$ symbolically, set the numerical precision to 25 digits and calculate the numerical value of the same expression. We finish by checking the current level of numerical accuracy.

>> **sym(1/2+1/3)**

ans =

5/6

>> **digits(25)**
vpa('1/2+1/3')

ans =

.8333333333333333333333333

>> **digits**

digits = 25

In the following example the ASCII characters whose numeric codes are 93, 126 and 115 are obtained.

>> **char (93,126,115)**

ans =

]
~
s

The following example transforms the series expansion of $\ln(1 + x)$ into Latex code, C code and FORTRAN code

>> **syms x**
>> **f = taylor(log(1+x));**
>> **latex(f)**

ans =

x-1/2\,{x}^{2}+1/3\,{x}^{3}-1/4\,{x}^{4}+1/5\,{x}^{5}

```
>> ccode(f)
```

ans =

A = x-x*x/2.0+x*x*x/3.0-x*x*x*x/4.0+x*x*x*x*x/5.0;

```
>> fortran(f)
```

ans =

A = x-x**2/2+x**3/3-x**4/4+x**5/5

Symbolic Functions. Substitution and Functional Operations

MATLAB's symbolic mathematics module allows you to define symbolic functions directly using the syntax $f = $ '*function*' (or $f = function$) provided the variables have previously been defined as symbolic with *syms*.

Once a symbolic function has been explicitly defined, it is possible to substitute values for the variables in the function, i.e., calculate the value of the function at a given point, using the commands shown below:

subs(f, a)	*Applies the function f at the point a.*
subs(f,a,b)	*Substitutes b in place of a in the function f.*
subs (f, variable, value)	*Replaces the* variable variable *by the* value value *in the function f.*
subs(f, {x,y,...}, {a,b,...})	*Replaces the variables {x, y,...} respectively by the values {a, b,...} in the function f.*

As a first example we define the function $f(x) = x^3$ and calculate $f(2)$ and $f(b+2)$.

```
>> f='x^3'
```

f =

x^3

```
>> A=subs(f,2)
```

A =

8

```
>> syms b
>> B=subs(f,b+2)
```

B =

(b+2) ^ 3

In the following example we consider the two-variable function $f(a, b) = a+b$ and first replace a by 4, and then a and b respectively by 3 and 5 (i.e., we find $f(3,5)$).

```
>> syms a b
>> subs(a+b,a,4)

ans =

4+b

>> subs(a+b,{a,b},{3,5})

ans =

8
```

Here are three additional examples of substitutions.

```
>> subs (cos (a) + (b), {a, b}, {sym ('alpha'), 2})

ans =

cos (alpha) + sin (2)

>> subs('exp(a*t)','a',-magic(2))

ans =

[exp (t),  exp(-3*t)]
[exp(-4*t), exp(-2*t)]

>> syms x y
>> subs(x*y,{x,y},{[0 1;-1 0],[1-1;-2 1]})

ans =

0-1
2 0
```

In addition to replacement, MATLAB also provides commands that allow functional operations, such as summation, subtraction, multiplication and division of functions, as well as composition and inversion. The following list summarizes the syntax of these commands:

symadd (f, g)	*Adds the functions f and g (f + g)*
symop(f, '+', g, '+', h, '+',.....)	*Returns the sum f+g+h +.... Note that symop is obsolete in more recent versions of MATLAB.*
symsub (f, g)	*Returns the difference of f and g (f-g)*
symop(f, '-', g, '-', h, '-',.....)	*Returns the difference f-g-h-...*
symmul (f, g)	*Returns the product of f and g (f * g)*

(continued)

symop(f, '*',g, '*', h, '*',.....)	*Returns the product f * g * h *...*
symdiv (f, g)	*Returns the quotient of f and g (f/g)*
symop(f, '/', g, '/', h, '/',.....)	*Returns the successive quotient((f/g)/h)/...*
sympow (f, k)	*Raises f to the power k (k a scalar)*
symop(f, '^',g)	*Raises a function to the power of another function (f^g)*
compose (f, g)	*Composes f and g (f ∘ g (x) = f (g (x)))*
compose(f, g, u)	*Composes f and g, taking the expression u as the domain of f and g*
g = finverse (f)	*Returns the inverse of the function f*
g = finverse(f, v)	*Returns the inverse of the function f using the symbolic variable v as an independent variable*

In the following example, given the functions $f(x)=x^2$, $g(x)=x^3+1$ and $h(x) = \sin(x)+\cos(x)$, we calculate $(f+g)(x)$, $(f-g+h)(x)$, $(f/g)(x)$, $f(g(x))$, $f(h(\pi/3))$ and $f(g(h(\sin(x))))$.

```
>> syms x
>> f = x ^ 2; g = x ^ 3 + 1; h = sin (x) + cos (x);
>> sum = symadd(f,g)
```

sum =

x^2+x^3+1

```
>> combination = symadd(symsub(f,g),h)
```

combination =

x ^ 2-x ^ 3-1 + sin (x) + cos (x)

```
>> combination = symop(f,'-',g,'+',h)
```

combination =

x ^ 2-x ^ 3-1 + sin (x) + cos (x)

```
>> quotient = symdiv (f, g)
```

quotient =

x ^ 2-/(x^3+1)

```
>> composite = subs (compose (g, f), x-1)
```

composite =

(x-1) ^ 6 + 1

```
>> composite1 = subs (compose (f, h), pi/3)
```

composite1 =

 1.8660

```
>> composite1 = subs (compose (f, h), ' pi/3')
```

composite1 =

(sin ((pi/3)) + cos ((pi/3))) ^ 2

```
>> composite2 = subs (compose (f , compose (g, h)), 'sin (x)')
```

composite2 =

((sin (sin (x)) + cos (sin (x))) ^ 3 + 1) ^ 2

In the following example we find the inverse of the function $f(x) = \sin(x^2)$ and check that the result is correct.

```
>> syms x
>> f = sin(x^2)
```

f =

sin(x^2)

```
>> g = finverse(f)
```

g =

asin(x)^(1/2)

```
>> compose(f,g)
```

ans =

x

MATLAB also provides a group of predefined symbolic special functions, whose syntax is presented in the following table:

cosint (x)	*The cosine integral,* $Ci(x) = \gamma + \ln(x) + \int_0^x \frac{\cos(t) - 1}{t} dt$
	where γ is the Euler–Mascheroni constant 0.5772156649...
sinint(x)	*The sine integral,* $Si(x) = \int_0^x \frac{\sin(t)}{t} dt$.
hypergeom(n,d,z)	*The generalized hypergeometric function.*
lambertw(x)	*The Lambert function $\lambda(x)$, which is defined by the equation $\lambda(x)e^{\lambda(x)} = x$.*
zeta(x)	*The Riemann zeta function $\zeta(x)$, defined as* $\zeta(x) = \sum_{k=1}^{\infty} \frac{1}{k^x}$.
zeta (n, x)	*The Nth derivative of zeta (x).*

As a first example we find the sum of the series $\sum_{k=1}^{\infty} \frac{1}{k^4}$, whose value is $\zeta(4)$.

```
>> zeta (4)
```

ans =

1.0823

Next we find the integral $\int_0^2 \frac{\sin(t)}{t} dt$. We use the sine integral function.

```
>> sinint (2)
```

ans =

  1.6054

Mathematical Analysis Functions. Limits, Continuity, and Series

MATLAB's symbolic mathematics module allows you to work on mathematical analysis with ease. It is possible to calculate limits, obtain derivatives, sum series, find the Taylor series of functions, calculate integrals and work with equations.

When working with limits, the same functions are applied to calculate limits of sequences, functions and sequences of functions, and of course, to analyze the continuity of functions and convergence of numerical series and power series. The analysis for one and several variables is similar. The following functions are available.

limit (sequence, inf)	*Calculates the limit of the sequence, indicated by its general term, as n tends to infinity.*
limit (sequence, inf)	*Calculates the limit of the sequence, indicated by its general term, as n tends to infinity.*
limit (function, x, a)	*Calculates the limit of the function of the variable x, indicated by its analytical expression, as the variable x tends towards the value a.*
limit (function, a)	*Calculates the limit of the function of the variable x, indicated by its analytical expression, as the variable x tends towards the value a.*
limit (function, x, a, 'right')	*Calculates the limit of the function of the variable x, indicated by its analytical expression, as the variable x tends to the value a from the right.*
limit (function, x, a, 'left')	*Calculates the limit of the function of the variable x, indicated by its analytical expression, as the variable x tends to the value a from the left.*
symsum (S, v, a, b)	*Finds the sum of the series with general term S where the variable v runs from a to b.*
symsum (S, v)	*Finds the sum of the series with general term S where the value of the variable v ranges from 0 to v-1.*
r = symsum (S)	*Returns the sum of the series with general term S in terms of the symbolic variable k (as determined by findsym) where the value of k ranges from 0 to k-1.*
symsum (S, a, b)	*Finds the sum of the series with general term S in terms of the symbolic variable k (as determined by findsym) where the value of k ranges from a to b.*

As a first example we calculate the following sequential limits:

$$\lim_{n\to\infty}\left(\frac{-3-2n}{-7+3n}\right)^4, \quad \lim_{n\to\infty}\frac{1+7n^2+3n^3}{5-8n+4n^3}, \quad \lim_{n\to\infty}\left(\frac{1+n}{2}\right)^4\frac{1+n}{n^5}, \quad \lim_{n\to\infty}\sqrt[n]{\frac{1+n}{n^2}}.$$

We have:

```
>> syms n
>> limit ((((2*n-3) /(3*n-7)) ^ 4, inf)

ans =

16/81

>> limit ((3*n^3+7*n^2+1) /(4*n^3-8*n+5), n, inf)

ans =

3/4

>> limit (((n+1)/2) * ((n^4+1)/n ^ 5), inf)

ans =

1/2
```

```
>> limit (((n+1)/n ^ 2) ^(1/n), inf)
```

ans =

1

Next we calculate the following function limits:

$$\lim_{x \to 1} \frac{-1+x}{-1+\sqrt{x}}, \quad \lim_{x \to 2} \frac{x-\sqrt{2+x}}{-3+\sqrt{1+4x}}, \quad \lim_{x \to 0} \sqrt[x]{1+x}, \quad \lim_{x \to 0} \frac{\sin((ax)^2)}{x^2}.$$

We have:

```
>> syms x a
>> limit((x-1)/(x^(1/2)-1),x,1)
```

ans =

2

```
>> limit((x-(x+2)^(1/2))/((4*x+1)^(1/2)-3),2)
```

ans =

9/8

```
>> limit((1+x)^(1/x))
```

ans =

exp (1)

```
>> limit(sin(a*x)^2/x^2,x,0)
```

ans =

a^2

In the following example we calculate the limit of the sequence of functions $g_n(x) = (x^2+nx)/n$ with $x \in \mathbf{R}$.

```
>> limit((x^2+n*x)/n,n,inf)
```

ans =

x

We see that the graph of the limit function is given by the diagonal passing through the first and third quadrants. We can demonstrate this as follows (see Figure 8-1):

```
>> fplot('[(x^2+x),(x^2+2*x)/2,(x^2+3*x)/3,(x^2+4*x)/4,
(x^2+5*x)/5,(x^2+5*x)/5,(x^2+6*x)/6,(x^2+7*x)/7,(x^2+8*x)/8,
(x^2+9*x)/9]',[-2,2,-2,2])
```

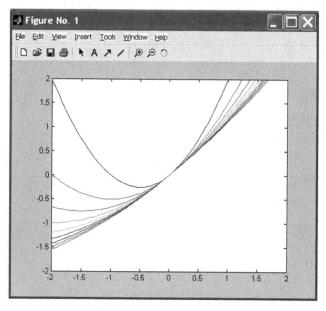

Figure 8-1.

The following example verifies the continuity of the function *f(x)* in **R**-{0} where *f(x)* = sin(*x*) /*x* . The following command checks that $\lim_{x \to a} f(x) = f(a)$.

```
>> syms x a
>> limit (sin (x) / x, x, a)
```

ans =

sin (a) /a

Next we show that the function $f(x) = \sqrt[x]{e}$ is not continuous at the point *x* = 0 by showing that the lateral limits do not match (one is zero and the other is infinite).

```
>> syms x
>> limit((exp(1/x)),x,0,'right')
```

ans =

inf

```
>> limit((exp(1/x)),x,0, 'left')
```

ans =

0

In the following example we determine whether the series $\sum_{n=1}^{\infty} \dfrac{n}{2^n}$ is convergent by applying the ratio test ($\lim_{n\to\infty} \dfrac{a(n+1)}{a(n)} < 1$) and if it is, we calculate its sum.

```
>> syms n
>> f = n/2 ^ n
```

f =

n/(2^n)

```
>> limit (subs(f,n,n+1)/f, n, inf)
```

ans =

1/2

We see that the limit of the ratio of successive terms is less than 1, which means the series converges. We calculate its sum using the following:

```
>> symsum(f,n,1,inf)
```

ans =

2

Derivatives, Integrals and Differential Equations

We describe below the MATLAB functions which are used in mathematical analysis when dealing with derivatives, integrals and differential equations. We will begin with the differentiation-related functions.

diff('f', 'x')	*Returns the derivative of f with respect to x.*
syms x, diff(f, x)	*Returns the derivative of f with respect to x.*
diff('f', 'x', n)	*Returns the nth derivative of f with respect to x.*
syms x, diff(f, x, n)	*Returns the nth derivative of f with respect to x.*
r = taylor(f, n, v)	*Returns the MacLaurin series of order n-1 for the function f in the variable v.*
r = taylor(f)	*Returns the MacLaurin series of order 5 for the function f in the default variable.*
r = taylor(f, n, v, a)	*Returns the Taylor series of order n-1 for the function f in the variable v in a neighborhood of the point a.*
R = jacobian(w, v)	*Returns the Jacobian matrix of w with respect to v.*

Below are the integration-related functions:

syms x, int(f(x), x) or int('f(x)', 'x')	Computes the indefinite integral $\int f(x)dx$
int (int ('f(x, y)', 'x'), 'y'))	Calculates the double integral $\int\int f(x)dxdy$
(syms x y int (int (f(x, y), x), y))	Calculates the double integral $\int\int f(x)dxdy$
int (int (int (... int ('f (x, y..., z)', 'x'), 'y')...), 'z')	Calculates $\int\int...\int f(x,y,...z)dxdy...dz$
syms x y z **int (int (int (... int (f(x, y...z), x), y)...), z)**	Calculates $\int\int...\int f(x,y,...z)dxdy...dz$
syms x a b, int(f(x), x, a, b)	Calculates the definite integral $\int_a^b f(x)dx$
int('f(x)', 'x', 'a', 'b')	Calculates the definite integral $\int_a^b f(x)dx$
int (int ('f(x,y)', 'x', 'a', 'b'), 'y', 'c', 'd'))	Calculates the integral $\int_a^b\int_c^d f(x,y)dxdy$
syms x y a b c d, **(int (int (f(x,y), x, a, b), y, c, d))**	Calculates the integral $\int_a^b\int_c^d f(x,y)dxdy$
int (int (int (... int ('f(x, y,...,z)', 'x', 'a', 'b'), 'y', **'c', 'd'),...), 'z', 'e', 'f')**	Calculates the integral $\int_a^b\int_c^d...\int_e^f f(x,y,...z)dxdy...dz$
syms x y z a b c d e f, **int (int (int (... int (f(x, y,...,z), x, a, b),)))** **y, c, d),...), z, e, f)**	Calculates the integral $\int_a^b\int_c^d...\int_e^f f(x,y,...z)dxdy...dz$

The following table summarizes the functions related to differential equations:

dsolve('e', 'v')	Solves the differential equation e where v is the independent variable (if you don't specify 'v', the independent variable is by default x). It returns only explicit solutions.
dsolve('e', 'c', 'v')	Solves the differential equation e subject to the initial condition specified by c and where v is the independent variable.
dsolve('e', c1, c2,...,cn, v')	Solves the equation differential e subject to the initial conditions specified by c1,...,cn, where v is the independent variable.
dsolve('e', c1, c2,...,cn, v')	Solves the differential equation e subject to the specified initial conditions c1,..,cn, where v is the independent variable.
dsolve('e1', 'e2',..., 'en', c1, **'c2',..., 'cn', 'v')**	Solves the system of differential equations e1,...,en, subject to the specified initial conditions c1,...,cn, where v is the independent variable.
dsolve('e1, e2,..., en, c1, **c2,..., cn', 'v')**	Solves the system of differential equations e1,...,en subject to the specified initial conditions c1,...,cn where v is the independent variable.

As a first example, we calculate the derivative of the function ln(sin(2x)).

```
>> pretty(diff('log(sin(2*x))','x'))
```

```
2 cos (2 x)
---------
sin (2 x)
```

This derivative can be simplified:

```
>> pretty(simple(diff('log(sin(2*x))','x')))
```

```
2
--------
tan(2 x)
```

In the following example we calculate the first, second, third and fourth derivatives of the function $f(x) = 1/x$.

```
>> f='1/x';
[diff(f),diff(f,2),diff(f,3),diff(f,4),diff(f,5)]
```

```
ans =
```

```
[-1/x ^ 2, 2/x ^ 3, - 6/x ^ 4, 24/x ^ 5, - 120/x ^ 6]
```

Then, given the function $f(x, y) = \sin(xy) + \cos(xy^2)$, we calculate the following partial derivatives: $\partial f/\partial x, \partial f/\partial y, \partial^2 f/\partial x^2, \partial^2 f/\partial y^2, \partial^2 f/\partial x\partial y, \partial^2 f/\partial y\partial x$ y $\partial^4 f/\partial^2 x \partial^2 y$

```
>> syms x y
>> f = sin(x*y) + cos(x*y^2)
```

```
f =
```

```
sin(x*y) + cos(x*y^2)
```

```
>> diff(f,x)
```

```
ans =
```

```
cos(x*y) *-sin(x*y^2) * y ^ 2
```

```
>> diff(f,y)
```

```
ans =
```

```
cos(x*y) * x-2 * sin(x*y^2) * x * y
```

```
>> diff(diff(f,x),x)
```

```
ans =
```

```
-sin(x*y) * y ^ 2-cos(x*y^2) * y ^ 4
```

```
>> diff (diff(f,y), y)
```

ans =

-sin(x*y) * x ^ 2-4 * cos(x*y^2) * x ^ 2 * y ^ 2-2 * sin(x*y^2) * x

```
>> diff(diff(f,x),y)
```

ans =

-sin(x*y) * x * y + cos(x*y)-2 * cos(x*y^2) * x * y ^ 3-2 * sin(x*y^2) * y

```
>> diff(diff(f,y),x)
```

ans =

-sin(x*y) * x * y + cos(x*y)-2 * cos(x*y^2) * x * y ^ 3-2 * sin(x*y^2) * y

```
>> diff(diff(diff(diff(f,x),x),y,y))
```

ans =

sin(x*y) * y ^ 3 * x-3 * cos(x*y) * y ^ 2 + 2 * cos(x*y^2) * y ^ 7 * x + 6 * sin(x*y^2) * y ^ 5

Next we find the Taylor series up to order 10 of the function $1/(2-x)$ in a neighborhood of the point $x=1$:

```
>> syms x
>> f=1/(2-x)
```

f =

1/(2-x)

```
>> pretty(taylor(f,11,x,1))
```

$$x + (x - 1)^2 + (x - 1)^3 + (x - 1)^4 + (x - 1)^5 + (x - 1)^6 + (x - 1)^7$$

$$+ (x - 1)^8 + (x - 1)^9 + (x - 1)^{10}$$

The following example computes the integral $\int \frac{1}{x^2-1}dx$.

```
>> int('1/(x^2-1)','x')
```

ans =

-atanh (x)

The following example estimates the integral $\int a \ln(1+bx)dx$ for arbitrary parameters a and b.

```
>> syms x a b, pretty(simple(int(a*log(1+b*x),x)))
```

```
a (log(1 + b x) - 1) (1 + b x)
-------------------------------
b
```

The following example computes the double integral $\int\int a\ln(1+bx)dxdb$ where a is an arbitrary parameter.

```
>> syms x a b, pretty(simple(int(int(a*log(1+b*x),x),b)))
```

```
a (-dilog(1 + b x) + log(1 + b x) + log(1 + b x) x b - 1 - 2 b x - log(b))
```

The following example computes the triple integral $\int\int\int a\ln(1+bx)dxdba$.

```
>> syms x a b, pretty(simple(int(int(int(a*log(1+b*x),x),b),a)))
```

```
     2
1/2a(-dilog(1 + b x) + log(1 + b x) + log(1 + b x) x b - 1 - 2 b x - log(b))
```

We calculate $\int_0^1 a \ln(1+bx)dx$.

```
>> syms x a b, pretty (simple (int (a * log(1+b*x), x, 0, 1)))
```

```
ab + log(1+b)+ b log (1+b) - b
-------------------------------
              b
```

The following example computes $\int_0^1\int_2^3 a\ln(1+bx)dxdb$, where a is an arbitrary parameter.

```
>> syms x a b, pretty(simple(int(int(a*log(1+b*x),x,0,1),b,2,3)))
```

```
a (8 log (2) - 2 - dilog (4) - 3 log (3) + dilog (3))
```

In the following example we solve the first order first degree differential equation $y'(t) = ay(t)$ where a is an arbitrary parameter.

```
>> pretty(dsolve('Dy = a*y'))
```

```
C1 exp (a t)
```

Thus we see that the family of solutions turns out to be $y(t) = c_1 e^{at}$.
Now we solve the above differential equation with the initial condition $y(0) = b$.

```
>> pretty(dsolve('Dy = a*y', 'y(0) = b'))
```

```
b exp (a t)
```

143

Next we solve the first order second degree differential equation $y'^2(s) + y^2(s) = 1$ with the initial condition $y(0) = 0$.

```
>> y = dsolve ('(Dy) ^ 2 + y ^ 2 = 1', ' (0) = 0', y 's')
```

```
y =
```

```
[-sin (s)]
[sin (s)]
```

Now we solve the second order first degree differential equation $y''(t) = a^2 y'(t)$ with the initial conditions $y(0) = 1$ and $y'(\pi/a) = 0$.

```
>> pretty (dsolve ('D2y = - a ^ 2 * y ', 'y(0) = 1, Dy (pi/a) = 0'))
```

```
cos (a t)
```

Therefore, the solution is the function $y(t) = \cos(at)$.
In the following example we solve the system of equations: $x'(t) = y(t),\ y'(t) = -x(t)$.

```
>> [x, y] = dsolve('Dx = y', 'Dy =-x')
```

```
x =
```

```
cos (t) * C1 + sin (t) * C2
```

```
y =
```

```
-sin (t) * C1 + cos (t) * C2
```

Next we calculate the solution of the previous system of differential equations for the initial conditions $x(0) = 0$ and $y(0) = 1$.

```
>> [x, y] = dsolve ('Dx = y, Dy = - x', 'x (0) = 0, y (0) = 1')
```

```
x =
```

```
sin (t)
```

```
y =
```

```
cos (t)
```

Linear Algebra: Simplifying and Solving Equations

Calculations with simple, rational and complex algebraic expressions are specially treated in MATLAB. The *Symbolic Match* toolbox functions efficiently implement the operations of simplification, factorization, grouping and expansion of algebraic expressions, and includes trigonometric expressions and expressions in a complex variable. The syntax of these functions is as follows.

r = collect(S) **r = collect(S, v)**	*Each polynomial in the array of polynomials S is grouped in terms of the variable v (or x if v is not specified).*
r = expand (S)	*Expands each polynomial or trigonometric, exponential or logarithmic function contained in S.*
factor(x)	*Factors x (symbolic or numerical).*
r = horner (p)	*Converts the polynomial p into its Horner, or nested, polynomial representation.*
[n, d] = numden (A)	*Converts each element of the symbolic or numerical matrix A to a simplified rational form.*
r = simple(s) **[r,how] = simple(s)**	*Simplifies the symbolic expression s looking for the shortest possible output. The second option presents only the final result and a string describing the particular simplification.*
r = simplify (S)	*Simplifies each element of the symbolic matrix S.*
[y, sigma] = **subexpr (x, sigma)** **[y, sigma] =** **subexpr (x, 'sigma')**	*Rewrites the symbolic expression x in terms of a common subexpression, substituting this subexpression with the symbolic variable sigma.*

As a first example we group the expression $y(\sin(x) + 1) + \sin(x)$ in terms of $\sin(x)$.

```
>> syms x and
>> pretty (collect (y * (sin (x) + 1) + sin (x), sin (x)))
```

(y + 1) sin (x) + y

Next we group, firstly in terms of x, and then $\ln(x)$, the function $f(x) = a\ln(x)-x\ln(x)-x$.

```
>> syms a x
>> f=a*log(x)-log(x)*x-x
```

f =

a*log(x)-log(x)*x-x

```
>> pretty(collect(f,x))
```

(- log (x) - 1) x + log (x)

```
>> pretty(collect(f,log(x)))
```

(a - x) log (x) - x

In the following example we expand various algebraic expressions.

```
>> syms a b x y t
>> expand([sin(2*t), cos(2*t)])
```

ans =

[2 * sin (t) * cos (t), 2 * cos (t) ^ 2-1]

>> **expand(exp((a+b)^2))**

ans =

*exp(a^2) * exp(a*b) ^ 2 * exp(b^2)*

>> **expand (cos (x + y))**

ans =

*cos (x) * cos (y) - sin (x) * sin(y)*

>> **expand((x-2)*(x-4))**

ans =

x^2-6*x+8

Next we factorize various expressions.

>> **factor(x^3-y^3)**

ans =

(x - y) *(x^2+x*y+y^2)

>> **factor([a^2-b^2, a^3+b^3])**

ans =

[(a-b)*(a+b), (a+b)*(a^2-a*b+b^2)]

>> **factor(sym('123456789012345 67890'))**

ans =

*(2) * (3) ^ 2 * (5) * (101) * (3803) * (3607) * (27961) * (3541)*

Below we simplify various expressions.

>> **syms x y z a b c**
>> **simplify(exp(c*log(sqrt(a+b))))**

ans =

(a + b) ^(1/2*c)

>> **simplify (sin (x) ^ 2 + cos (x) ^ 2)**

ans =

1

146

```
>> S = [(x^2+5*x+6)/(x+2),sqrt(16)];
R = simplify(S)
```

R =

[x+3,   4]

The following functions can be used to solve symbolic equations and systems of equations:

solve('equation', 'x')	*Solves the equation in terms of the variable x.*
syms x; solve(equation,x)	*Solve the equation in terms of the variable x.*
solve('e1,e2,...,en', 'x1,x2,...,xn')	*Solves the system of equations e1,...,en in terms of the variables x1,..., xn.*
syms x1 x2... xn; **solve(e1,e2,...,en, x1,x2,...,xn)**	*Solves the system of equations e1,...,en in terms of the variables x1,..., xn.*

As a first example we solve the equation $3ax - 7x^2 + x^3 = 0$ in terms of x, where a is a parameter.

```
>> solve('3*a*x-7*x^2+x^3=0','x')
```

ans =

```
[                       0]
[7/2 + 1/2 *(49-12*a) ^(1/2)]
[7/2-1/2 *(49-12*a) ^(1/2)]
```

Next we solve the above equation where a is the variable and x is the parameter.

```
>> pretty(solve('3*a*x-7*x^2+x^3=0','a'))
```

-1/3 x (- 7 + x)

In the following example, we calculate the fourth roots of -1 and 1.

```
>> S=solve('x^4+1=0')
```

S =

```
[  1/2*2^(1/2)+1/2*i*2^(1/2)]
[ -1/2*2^(1/2)-1/2*i*2^(1/2)]
[  1/2*2^(1/2)-1/2*i*2^(1/2)]
[ -1/2*2^(1/2)+1/2*i*2^(1/2)]
```

```
>> numeric(S)
```

ans =

```
0.70710678118655 + 0.70710678118655i
-0.70710678118655 - 0.70710678118655i
0.70710678118655 - 0.70710678118655i
-0.70710678118655 + 0.70710678118655i
```

147

```
>> S1=solve('x^4-1=0')
```

S1 =

```
[  1]
[ -1]
[  i]
[ -i]
```

Next we calculate the fifth roots of the complex number 2 + 2*i*.

```
>> numeric(solve('x^5-(2+2*i)=0'))
```

ans =

```
1.21598698264961 + 0. 19259341768888i
0.19259341768888 + 1. 215986982649961i
-1.09695770450838 + 0. 558927867466011i
-0.87055056329612 - 0. 870550563296121i
0.55892786746601 1. 09695770450838i
```

In the following example we solve the equation sin(*x*)cos(*x*)=*a* in the variable *x*:

```
>> simple (solve ('sin (x) * cos (x) = a', 'x'))
```

ans =

```
 pi/2 - asin(2*a)/2
        asin(2*a)/2
```

```
>> pretty(ans)
```

```
 +-                 -+
 |  pi    asin(2 a)  |
 |  -- - ---------   |
 |  2        2       |
 |                   |
 |      asin(2 a)    |
 |      ---------    |
 |          2        |
 +-                 -+
```

If we solve the above equation for the particular case *a*= 0 we get:

```
>> solve ('sin (x) * cos (x) = 0', 'x')
```

ans =

```
[       0]
[1/2 * pi]
[-1/2 * pi]
```

In the following example we solve the system $u + v + w = a$, $3u + v = b$, $u - 2v - w = 0$, where u, v and w are variables and a, b and c parameters.

```
>> syms u v w a b c
>> [u, v, w] = solve('u+v+w=a,3*u+v=b,u-2*v-w=c',u,v,w)

u =

1/5 * b + 1/5 * + 1/5 * c

v =

2/5 * b-3/5 * a-3/5 * c

w =

-3/5 * b + 7/5 * + 2/5 * c
```

EXERCISE 8-1

Consider the symbolic matrix A below:

$$\begin{bmatrix} a & b & c \\ 3c & a-3c & b \\ 3b & -3b+3c & a-3c \end{bmatrix}$$

Calculate A', A⁻¹, determinant (A), trace (A), range (A).

We start by defining the symbolic matrix of our problem as follows:

```
>> A=sym('[a,b,c; 3*c,a-3*c,b; 3*b,-3*b+3*c,a-3*c]')

A =

[   a,       b,       c]
[ 3*c,    a-3*c,      b]
[ 3*b,-3*b+3*c,a-3*c]
```

Alternatively, the same symbolic matrix can be defined by previously declaring all the variables as symbolic as follows:

```
>> syms a b c
>> A=sym([a,b,c; 3*c,a-3*c,b; 3*b,-3*b+3*c,a-3*c])

A =

[      a,        b,        c]
[    3*c,     a-3*c,       b]
[    3*b,  -3*b+3*c,    a-3*c]
```

149

>> transpose (A)

ans =

```
[a, 3 * c, * 3B]
[b, a-3*c, -3*b+3*c]
[c,    b,    a-3*c]
```

>> pretty(inv(A))

```
    2               2     2
[ a  - 6 a c + 9 c  + 3 b  - 3 b c       a b - 3 c        - b  + a c - 3 c ]
[ ----------------------------       ------------       --------------- ]
[               %1                         %1                  %1        ]
[                                                                        ]
[        2            2       2                                          ]
[     - b  + a c - 3 c      a  - 3 a c - 3 b c        a b - 3 c          ]
[   - 3 ---------------      -----------------      - ----------         ]
[             %1                   %1                      %1            ]
[                                                                        ]
[                2                      2      2                         ]
[        a b - 3 c            a b - a c + b       a  - 3 a c - 3 b c     ]
[     - 3 ----------        3 ---------------      ----------------      ]
[             %1                   %1                   %1               ]
```

```
         3       2      2        2        3     3       2
%1 :=  a  - 6 c a  + 9 c  a + 3 a b  - 9 a b c + 9 c  + 3 b  + 9 b c
```

>> pretty(det(A))

```
 3       2      2        2        3     3       2
a  - 6 c a  + 9 c  a + 3 a b  - 9 a b c + 9 c  + 3 b  + 9 b c
```

>> pretty(trace (A))

3 a - 6 c

>> rank(A)

ans =

3

>> A^2

ans =

```
[ a^2+6*b*c,            a*b+b*(a-3*c)+c*(-3*b+3*c), a*c+b^2+c*(a-3*c)]
[3*a*c+3*c*(a-3*c)+3*b^2, 3*b*c+(a-3*c)^2+b*(-3*b+3*c), 3*c^2+2*b*(a-3*c)]
[3*a*b+3*c*(-3*b+3*c)+3*b*(a-3*c), 3*b^2+2*(-3*b+3*c)*(a-3*c), 3*b*c+(a-3*c)^2+b*(-3*b+3*c)]
```

```
                              EXERCISE 8-2
```

Find the intersection of the hyperbolas with equations $x^2 - y^2 = 1$ and $y^2x^2 - b^2y^2 = 16$ with the parabola $z^2 = 2x$.

We solve the system of three equations as follows:

```
>> [x, y, z] = solve('a^2*x^2-b^2*y^2=16','x^2-y^2=1','z^2=2*x', 'x,y,z')
```

x =

```
[   1/2*(((b^2-16)/(a^2-b^2))^(1/4)+i*((b^2-16)/(a^2-b^2))^(1/4))^2]
[   1/2*(((b^2-16)/(a^2-b^2))^(1/4)+i*((b^2-16)/(a^2-b^2))^(1/4))^2]
[  1/2*(-((b^2-16)/(a^2-b^2))^(1/4)+i*((b^2-16)/(a^2-b^2))^(1/4))^2]
[  1/2*(-((b^2-16)/(a^2-b^2))^(1/4)+i*((b^2-16)/(a^2-b^2))^(1/4))^2]
[   1/2*(((b^2-16)/(a^2-b^2))^(1/4)-i*((b^2-16)/(a^2-b^2))^(1/4))^2]
[   1/2*(((b^2-16)/(a^2-b^2))^(1/4)-i*((b^2-16)/(a^2-b^2))^(1/4))^2]
[  1/2*(-((b^2-16)/(a^2-b^2))^(1/4)-i*((b^2-16)/(a^2-b^2))^(1/4))^2]
[  1/2*(-((b^2-16)/(a^2-b^2))^(1/4)-i*((b^2-16)/(a^2-b^2))^(1/4))^2]
```

y =

```
[   1/(a^2-b^2)*(-(a^2-b^2)*(a^2-16))^(1/2)]
[  -1/(a^2-b^2)*(-(a^2-b^2)*(a^2-16))^(1/2)]
[   1/(a^2-b^2)*(-(a^2-b^2)*(a^2-16))^(1/2)]
[  -1/(a^2-b^2)*(-(a^2-b^2)*(a^2-16))^(1/2)]
[   1/(a^2-b^2)*(-(a^2-b^2)*(a^2-16))^(1/2)]
[  -1/(a^2-b^2)*(-(a^2-b^2)*(a^2-16))^(1/2)]
[   1/(a^2-b^2)*(-(a^2-b^2)*(a^2-16))^(1/2)]
[  -1/(a^2-b^2)*(-(a^2-b^2)*(a^2-16))^(1/2)]
```

z =

```
[   ((b^2-16)/(a^2-b^2))^(1/4)+i*((b^2-16)/(a^2-b^2))^(1/4)]
[   ((b^2-16)/(a^2-b^2))^(1/4)+i*((b^2-16)/(a^2-b^2))^(1/4)]
[  -((b^2-16)/(a^2-b^2))^(1/4)+i*((b^2-16)/(a^2-b^2))^(1/4)]
[  -((b^2-16)/(a^2-b^2))^(1/4)+i*((b^2-16)/(a^2-b^2))^(1/4)]
[   ((b^2-16)/(a^2-b^2))^(1/4)-i*((b^2-16)/(a^2-b^2))^(1/4)]
[   ((b^2-16)/(a^2-b^2))^(1/4)-i*((b^2-16)/(a^2-b^2))^(1/4)]
[  -((b^2-16)/(a^2-b^2))^(1/4)-i*((b^2-16)/(a^2-b^2))^(1/4)]
[  -((b^2-16)/(a^2-b^2))^(1/4)-i*((b^2-16)/(a^2-b^2))^(1/4)]
```

EXERCISE 8-3

Evaluate the following integrals:

$$\int_{-3}^{3} \frac{1}{3} \frac{\sin(2t)}{t} dt, \quad \int_{0}^{5} \frac{\cos(x)-1}{x} dx.$$

For the first integral the integrand is an even function, so our integral between -3 and 3 will be twice the integral between 0 and 3. Then we make the change of variable $2t = v$, and arrive at the integral:

$$\int_{-3}^{3} \frac{1}{3} \frac{\sin(2t)}{t} dt = 2\int_{0}^{3} \frac{1}{3} \frac{\sin(2t)}{t} dt = \frac{2}{3}\int_{0}^{6} \frac{\sin(v)}{v} dv$$

whose solution by MATLAB is as follows:

```
>> (2/3) * (sinint (6))
```

ans =

   0.9498

To calculate the second integral we have in mind the following:

$$Ci(x) = \gamma + \ln(x) + \int_{0}^{x} \frac{\cos(t)-1}{t} dt \Rightarrow \int_{0}^{5} \frac{\cos(x)-1}{x} dx = Ci(5) - \gamma + \ln(5)$$

which can be calculated in MATLAB as follows:

```
>> cosint(5) - 0.577215664-log(5)
```

ans =

   -2.3767

EXERCISE 8-4

Given the function h defined by $h(x,y) = (cos(x^2-y^2), sin(x^2-y^2))$, calculate $h(1,2)$, $h(-\pi,\pi)$ and $h(cos(a^2), cos(1-a^2))$.

We create a vector of two functions as follows:

```
>> syms x y a.
>> h = [cos(x^2-y^2), sin(x^2-y^2)]
```

h =

[cos(x^2-y^2), sin(x^2-y^2)]

Now we calculate the requested values:

>> **subs(h,{x,y},{1,2})**

ans =

-0.9900-0.1411

>> **subs(h,{x,y},{-pi,pi})**

ans =

   1 0

>> **subs (h, {x, y}, {cos(a^2), cos(1-a^2)})**

ans =

[cos (cos(a^2) ^ 2-cos(-1+a^2) ^ 2), sin (cos(a^2) ^ 2-cos(-1+a^2) ^ 2)]

EXERCISE 8-5

Given the function *f* defined by:

$$f(x,y) = 3(1-x)^2 e^{-(y+1)^2 - x^2} - 10\left(\frac{1}{5}x - x^3 - \frac{1}{5}y\right)e^{-x^2 - y^2} - \frac{1}{3}e^{-(x+1)^2 - y^2}$$

find *f* (0,0) and represent *f* graphically.

In this case, since it is necessary to represent the function graphically, we define it in the M-file shown in Figure 8-2.

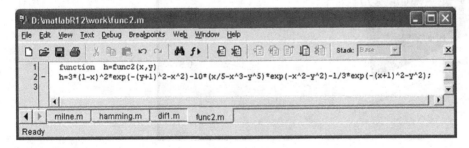

Figure 8-2.

Now we calculate the value of *f* at *(0,0)*:

>> *func2 (0,0)*

ans =

0.9810

To create the graph of the function (in a neighborhood of the origin), we use the command *meshgrid* to define the surface characteristics, and the command *surf* to draw the surface:

```
>> [x, y] = meshgrid(-0.5:.05:0.5,-0.5:.05:0.5);
>> z = func2(x,y);
>> surf (x, y, z)
```

This yields the graph shown in Figure 8-3:

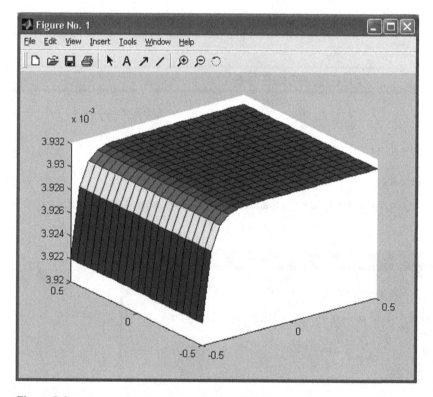

Figure 8-3.

EXERCISE 8-6

Given the functions $f(x) = \sin(\cos(x^{1/2}))$ and $g(x) = \mathrm{sqrt}(\tan(x^2))$ calculate the composite of f and g and the composite of g and f. Also calculate the inverses of f and g.

```
>> syms x, f = sin (cos (x ^(1/2)));
>> g=sqrt(tan(x^2));
>> simple(compose(f,g))
```

ans =

sin (cos (tan(x^2) ^(1/4)))

```
>> simple (compose(g,f))
```

ans =

tan (sin (cos (x ^(1/2))) ^ 2) ^(1/2)

```
>> F = finverse (f)
```

F =

acos (asin (x)) ^ 2

```
>> G = finverse (g)
```

G =

atan(x^2) ^(1/2)

EXERCISE 8-7

Define the function *f(x)* as:

$$f(x) = \frac{1}{1 + \sqrt[x]{e}} \text{ if } x \neq 0 \text{ and } f(x) = 1 \text{ if } x = 0$$

and study its continuity on the real line.

Except at the point $x = 0$ the continuity is clear. To analyze the behavior of the function at the point $x = 0$ we calculate the lateral limits as $x \rightarrow 0$:

```
>> syms x
limit(1/(1+exp(1/x)),x,0,'right')
```

ans =

0

155

```
>> limit(1/(1+exp(1/x)),x,0,'left')
```

ans =

1

The limit of the function as $x \to 0$ does not exist because the lateral limits are different. But, since the lateral limits are finite, the discontinuity at $x = 0$ is a finite jump (also known as a discontinuity of the first kind). We illustrate this result in the graph shown in Figure 8-4.

```
>> fplot('1/(1+exp(1/x))',[-5,5])
```

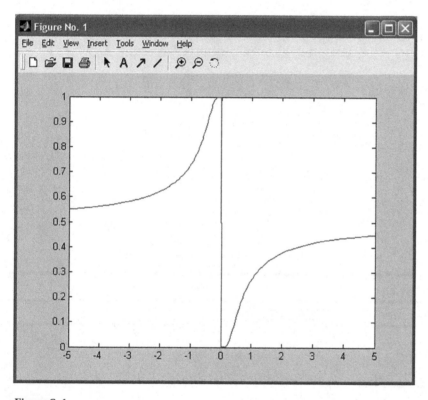

Figure 8-4.

EXERCISE 8-8

Study the continuity of the function $f: R^2 \to R$ defined by:

$$f(x,y) = \frac{(x-1)^2 y^2}{(x-1)^2 + y^2} \text{ if } (x,y) \neq (1,0) \text{ and } f(1,0) = 0.$$

Since the function is clearly continuous elsewhere, we only need to check the continuity of the function at (1,0). We need to show that.

$$\lim_{(x,y) \to (1,0)} f(x,y) = 0.$$

» **syms x y m a r**
» **limit (limit (y ^ 2 *(x-1) ^ 2 / (y ^ 2 +(x-1) ^ 2), x, 0), y, 0)**

ans =

0

» **limit (limit (y ^ 2 *(x-1) ^ 2 / (y ^ 2 + (x-1) ^ 2), y, 0), x, 0)**

ans =

0

» **limit((m*x)^2*(x-1)^2/((m*x)^2+(x-1)^2),x,0)**

ans=

0

» **limit ((m*x) *(x-1) ^ 2/((m*x) +(x-1) ^ 2), x, 0)**

ans =

0

Thus we see that the iterated and directional limits (along the lines $y = mx$) coincide, which leads us to believe that the limit exists and that its value is zero. To corroborate these results we calculate the limit in polar coordinates:

» **limit (limit ((r ^ 2 * sin (a) ^ 2) * (r * cos (a) - 1) ^ 2 / ((r ^ 2 * sin (a) ^ 2) + (r * cos (a) - 1) ^ 2), r, 1), a, 0)**

ans =

0

We conclude that the limit is zero at the point (1,0), which ensures the continuity of the function. In Figure 8-5 we graph the surface defined by f, and in particular illustrate the continuity and the tendency to 0 of the function in a neighborhood of the point (1,0).

```
» [x, y] = meshgrid(0:0.05:2,-2:0.05:2);
z=y.^2.*(x-1).^2./(y.^2+(x-1).^2);
mesh(x,y,z), view ([- 23, 30])
```

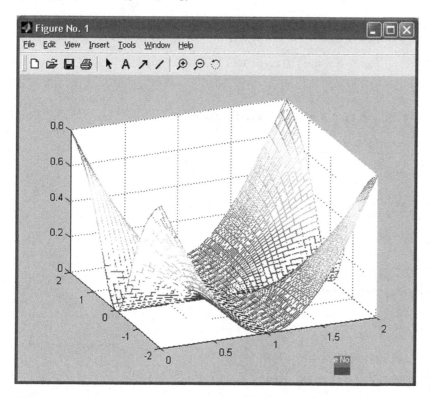

Figure 8-5.

EXERCISE 8-9

Find the sum of each of the following series:

$$\sum_{n=2}^{\infty}\frac{3+2n}{7^{n}n(1+n)},$$

$$\sum_{n=1}^{\infty}\frac{n}{p^{n}},$$

where p is a parameter.

Before finding the sums we first need to determine whether the series do indeed converge. We apply the ratio test for the first series:

```
>> syms n
>> f=(3+2*n)/((1-n)*n*7^n);
>> pretty(f)
```

$$3 + 2\ n$$

$$n$$
$$(1 - n)\ n\ 7$$

```
>> limit(subs(f,n,n+1)/f,n,inf)
```

ans =

1/7

As the limit is less than 1, the series is convergent. We will calculate its sum. The result MATLAB returns will often be complicated and depend on certain special functions. We obtain the following:

```
>> S1 = symsum(f,n,2,inf)
```

S1 =

-6 * log(6/7)-22/21 + 13/343 * hypergeom([2, 2],[3],1/7)

Now we apply the ratio test for the second series.

```
>> syms n p
>> g=n/p^n;
>> pretty(g)
```

$$n$$

$$n$$
$$p$$

```
>> limit(subs(g,n,n+1)/g,n,inf)
```

ans =

1/p

Thus, if $p > 1$, the series converges, and if $p < 1$, the series diverges, and if $p = 1$, we get the series with general term n, which diverges. When p is greater than 1, we can find the sum of the series:

```
>> S2=symsum(g,n,2,inf)
```

S2 =

```
2/p^2*(1/2/(-1+p)^3*p^4*(-1/p+1)-1/2*p)
```

```
>> pretty(simple(S2))
```

```
-1 + 2 p
-----------
          2
p (- 1 + p)
```

EXERCISE 8-10

Find the MaClaurin series of order 13 of the function sinh*(x)*. Also find the Taylor series of order 6 of the function $1/(1+x)$ in a neighborhood of the point $x = 1$.

```
>> pretty(taylor(sinh(x),13))
```

```
        3           5           7            9              11
x + 1/6 x  + 1/120 x  + 1/5040 x  + 1/362880 x  + 1/39916800 x
```

```
>> pretty(taylor(1/(1+x),6,1))
```

```
                      2            3            4            5
3/4 - 1/4 x + 1/8 (x - 1)  - 1/16 (x - 1)  + 1/32 (x - 1)  - 1/64 (x - 1)
```

EXERCISE 8-11

Study the function

$$f(x) = \frac{x^3}{x^2 - 1}$$

calculating the asymptotes, maxima, minima, inflexion points, intervals of growth and decrease and intervals of concavity and convexity.

```
>> f='x ^ 3 /(x^2-1)'
```

f =

```
x ^ 3 /(x^2-1)
```

```
>> syms x, limit (x ^ 3 /(x^2-1), x, inf)
```

ans =

NaN

Thus, there are no horizontal asymptotes. To see if there are vertical asymptotes, we look at the values of x that make y infinite:

```
>> solve('x^2-1')
```

ans =

[1]
[-1]

The vertical asymptotes are the lines $x = 1$ and $x =-1$. Now let us see if there are any oblique asymptotes:

```
>> limit(x^3/(x^2-1)/x,x,inf)
```

ans =

1

```
>> limit(x^3/(x^2-1)-x,x,inf)
```

ans =

0

The line $y = x$ is an oblique asymptote. Now we will analyze the maxima and minima, inflection points and intervals of concavity and growth of the function:

```
>> solve (diff (f))
```

ans =

[0]
[0]
[3 ^(1/2)]
[^(1/2) - 3]

The first derivative vanishes at $x = 0$, $x=\sqrt{3}$ and $x=\sqrt{3}$. These include maximum and minimum candidates. To verify if they are maxima or minima, we find the value of the second derivative at those points:

```
>> [numeric(subs(diff(f,2),0)),numeric(subs(diff(f,2),sqrt(3))),
numeric(subs(diff(f,2),-sqrt(3)))]
```

ans =

0 2.5981 - 2.5981

Therefore, at the point with abscissa $x=\sqrt{3}$ there is a maximum and at the point with abscissa $x=\sqrt{3}$ there is a minimum. At $x = 0$ we know nothing:

```
>> [numeric (subs (f, sqrt (3))), numeric (subs (f, - sqrt (3)))]
```

ans =

2.5981 - 2.5981

Therefore, the maximum is at (-√3, -2.5981) and the minimum is at √3, 2.5981).

We will now analyze the points of inflection:

```
>> solve(diff(f,2))
```

ans =

```
[         0]
[ i*3^(1/2)]
[-i * 3 ^(1/2)]
```

The only possible turning point occurs at $x = 0$, and as $f(0) = 0$, this possible turning point is (0,0):

```
>> subs (diff(f,3), 0)
```

ans =

-6

As the third derivative at $x = 0$ is not zero, we see that the origin is indeed a turning point:

```
>> pretty(simple(diff(f)))
```
$$\frac{x^2 (x^2 - 3)}{(x^2 - 1)^2}$$

The curve is increasing when $y' > 0$, i.e., in the intervals $(-\infty, -\sqrt{3})$ and $(\sqrt{3}, \infty)$.

The curve is decreasing when $y' < 0$, i.e., in the defined intervals $(-\sqrt{3},-1)$, $(-1,0)$, $(0,1)$ and $(1, \sqrt{3})$.

```
>> pretty(simple(diff(f,2)))
```
$$\frac{2 x (x^2 + 3)}{(x^2 - 1)^3}$$

The curve is concave when $y'' > 0$, i.e., in the intervals *(-1,0)* and *(1, ∞)*.

The curve is convex when $y'' < 0$, i.e. in the intervals *(0,1)* and *(- ∞ , - 1)*.

The curve has a horizontal tangent at the three points at which the first derivative is zero. The equations of the horizontal tangents are $y = 0$, $y = 2.5981$ and $y = -2.5981$.

The curve has a vertical tangent at the points that make the first derivative infinite. These are $x = 1$ and $x = -1$. Therefore, the vertical tangents coincide with the two vertical asymptotes.

We graph the curve together with its asymptotes (see Figure 8-6):

```
>> fplot('[x^3/(x^2-1),x]',[-5,5,-5,5])
```

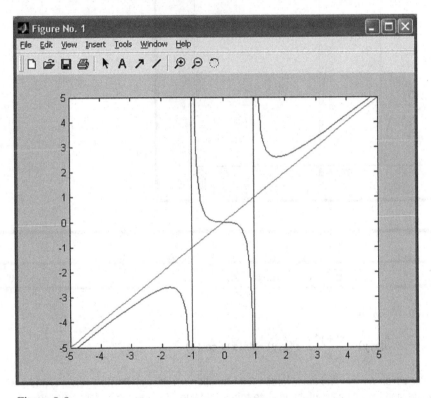

Figure 8-6.

We can also show the curve, its asymptotes and its horizontal and vertical tangents in the same graph (Figure 8-7):

```
>> fplot('[x^3/(x^2-1),x,2.5981,-2.5981]',[-5,5,-5,5])
```

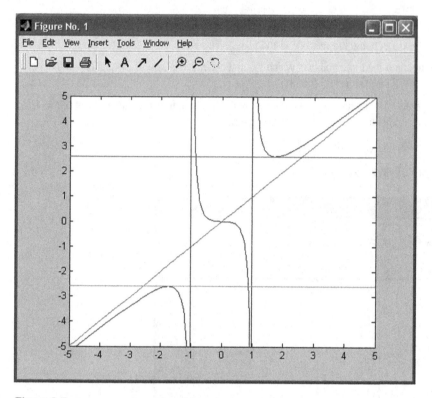

Figure 8-7.

EXERCISE 8-12

Given the vector function *(u(x,y), v(x,y))*, where:

$$u(x,y) = \frac{x^4 + y^4}{x}, \quad v(x,y) = \sin(x) + \cos(y)$$

determine the conditions under which we can find the inverse vector function *(x(u,v), y(u,v))* with *x = x(u, v)* and *y = y(u,v)* and find the derivative and the Jacobian of the inverse transformation. Find the value of this inverse function at the point *(π/4,-π/4)*.

To find the conditions under which the function is invertible we appeal to the inverse function theorem. The functions are differentiable with continuous derivatives, except perhaps at *x*= 0. Now we consider the Jacobian of the transformation ∂ *(u(x, y), v(x,y)) / ∂(x, y)*:

```
>> syms x y
>> J=simple((jacobian([(x^4+y^4)/x,sin(x)+cos(y)],[x,y])))

J =

[ 3*x^2-1/x^2*y^4,        4*y^3/x]
[         cos(x),        -sin(y)]
```

```
>> pretty(det(J))
```

$$\frac{3 \sin(y) \, x^4 - \sin(y) \, y^4 + 4 \, y^3 \cos(x) \, x}{x^2}$$

Therefore, at the points where this expression does not vanish, we can solve for *x* and *y* in terms of *u* and *v*. In addition, we must also have *x*≠0.

We calculate the derivative of the inverse function. Its value is the inverse of the Jacobian matrix of the original function found above and the determinant of its Jacobian is the reciprocal of the determinant of the Jacobian of the original function:

```
>> I=simple(inv(J));
>> pretty(simple(det(I)))
```

$$- \frac{x^2}{3 \sin(y) \, x^4 - \sin(y) \, y^4 + 4 \, y^3 \cos(x) \, x}$$

We now find the value of this inverse function at the point *(π/4,-π/4)*:

```
>> numeric(subs(subs(determ(I),pi/4,'x'),-pi/4,'y'))
```

ans =

0.38210611216717

```
>> numeric(subs(subs(symdiv(1,determ(J)),pi/4,'x'),-pi/4,'y'))
```

ans =

0.38210611216717

These results confirm that the determinant of the Jacobian of the inverse function is the reciprocal of the determinant of the Jacobian of the original function.

EXERCISE 8-13

Given the function $f(x,y)=e^{-(x+y)}$ and the transformation $u = u(x,y) = x + y$, $v = v(x,y) = x$, find $f(u,v)$.

We calculate the inverse transformation and its Jacobian to apply the change of variables theorem:

```
>> syms x y u v
>> [x,y]=solve('u=x+y,v=x','x','y')
```

x =

v

y =

u-v

```
>> jacobian([v,u-v],[u,v])
```

ans =

```
[  0,  1]
[  1, -1]
```

```
>> f=exp(x-y);
>> pretty(simple(subs(f,{x,y},{v,u-v})* abs(det(jacobian(
[v,u-v],[u,v])))))
exp(2 v - u)
```

The requested function is $f(u,v)= e^{2v-u}$.

EXERCISE 8-14

Find the following integrals:

$$\int\frac{dx}{x^3\sqrt{x^2+3x-1}}, \quad \int\frac{\sqrt{9-4x^2}}{x}dx, \quad \int x^8(3+5x^3)^{\frac{1}{4}}dx.$$

```
>> syms x
>> pretty(simple(int(x^(-3)*(x^2+3*x-1)^(-1/2),x)))
```

```
            2          1/2        2          1/2
         (x  + 3 x - 1)        (x  + 3 x - 1)
   1/2 ------------------ + 9/4 ------------------
               2                       x
              x
```

$$+ 31/8\ atan(1/2\ \frac{-2 + 3\ x}{(x^2 + 3\ x - 1)^{1/2}})$$

```
>> pretty(simple(int(x^(-1)*(9-4*x^2)^(1/2), x)))
```

$$(9 - 4\ x^2)^{1/2} - 3\ atanh(\frac{3}{(9 - 4\ x^2)^{1/2}})$$

```
>> pretty(simple(int(x^8*(3+5*x^3)^(1/4),x)))
```

$$4/73125\ (288 - 120\ x^3 + 125\ x^6 + 1875\ x^9)\ (3 + 5\ x^3)^{1/4}$$

EXERCISE 8-15

Consider the following curve, given in polar coordinates, $r = 3-3cos\ (a)$. Calculate the length of the arc corresponding to one complete revolution ($0\le a\le 2\pi$).

```
>> r='3-3*cos(a)';
>> diff(r,'a')
```

ans =

3 * sin (a)

```
>> R = simple (int ('((3-3 * cos (a)) ^ 2 + (3 * sin (a)) ^ 2) ^(1/2) ',' a ', ' 0','2 * pi'))
```

R =

24

EXERCISE 8-16

Calculate the value of the following integral:

$$\int_{-1.96}^{1.96} \frac{e^{\frac{x^2}{2}}}{\sqrt{2\pi}}\,dx$$

which represents the area under the normal curve between the specified limits.

```
>> numeric(int('exp(-x^2/2)/(2*pi)^(1/2)','x',-1.96,1.96))
```

ans =

0.95000420970356

EXERCISE 8-17

Find the intersection of the surfaces $ax^2 + y^2 = z$ and $z = a^2 - y^2$ and calculate the volume enclosed in the intersection. Also find the volume enclosed in the intersection of the surfaces $z = x^2$ and $4 - y^2 = z$.

The first volume is calculated by means of the integral:

```
>> pretty(simple(int(int(int('1','z','a*x^2+y^2',
'a^2-y^2'),'y',0,'sqrt((a^2-a*x^2)/2)'),'x',0,'sqrt(a)')))
        /
        |                  2    2       2 1/2
  1/24  |    lim       3 a  x (2 a  - 2 a x )
        |        1/2
        \x -> (a   )-


                         1/2 1/2                           \
           7/2  1/2      2   a   x                 2      2 3/2|
      + 3 a    2    atan(------------------) + x (2 a  - 2 a x )   |
                          2      2 1/2                        |
                       (2 a  - 2 a x )                        /
```

To calculate the second volume we first produce a graph of the requested intersection, with the aim of clarifying the limits of integration, using the following syntax:

```
>> [x, y] = meshgrid(-2:.1:2);
z = x ^ 2;
mesh(x,y,z)
hold on;
z = 4 - y. ^ 2;
mesh (x, y, z)
```

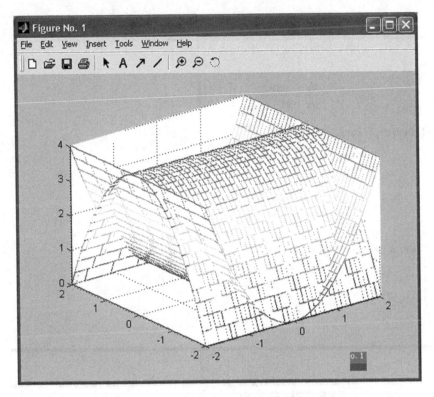

Figure 8-8.

Now we can find the requested volume by calculating the following integral:

```
>> pretty(simple(int(int(int('1','z','x^2','4-y^2'),
'y',0,'sqrt(4-x^2)'),'x',0,2)))
```

2 pi

EXERCISE 8-18

Solve the following equation:

$$\frac{dy}{dx} = \frac{xy}{y^2 - x^2}.$$

```
>> pretty(simple(dsolve('Dy=(x*y)/(y^2-x^2)')))
```

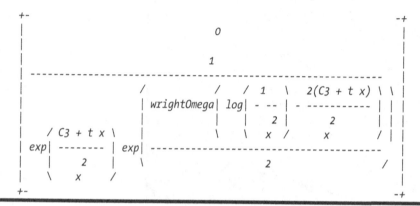

EXERCISE 8-19

Solve the following equations:

$$9y'''' - 6y''' + 46y'' - 6y' + 37y = 0$$
$$3y'' + 2y' - 5y = 0$$
$$2y'' + 5y' + 5y = 0$$

where $y(0) = 0$ and $y'(0) = \frac{1}{2}$.

```
>> pretty(simple(dsolve('9*D4y-6*D3y+46*D2y-6*Dy+37*y=0')))
```

C1 sin(t) + C2 cos(t) + C3 exp(1/3 t) sin(2 t) + C4 exp(1/3 t) cos(2 t)

```
>> pretty(dsolve('3*D2y+2*Dy-5*y=0'))
```

C1 exp(t) + C2 exp(- 5/3 t)

```
>> pretty(dsolve('2*D2y+5*Dy+5*y=0','y(0)=0,Dy(0)=1/2'))
```

```
          1/2                      1/2
    2/15 15    exp(- 5/4 t) sin(1/4 15    t)
```

EXERCISE 8-20

Subject to the initial conditions $x(0) = 1$ and $y(0) = 2$, solve the following system of equations:

$$x' - y = e\text{-}t$$
$$y' + 5\,x + 2\,y = \sin\ (3t).$$

`>> [x,y]=dsolve('Dx-Dy=exp(-t),Dy+5*x+2*y=sin(3+t)','x(0)=1,y(0)=2','t')`

x =

(-7/50*sin(3)+1/50*cos(3)+7/6)*exp(-7*t)+7/50*sin(3+t)-1/50*cos(3+t)-1/6*exp(-t)

y =

(-7/50*sin(3)+1/50*cos(3)+7/6)*exp(-7*t)+5/6*exp(-t)+7/50*sin(3+t)-1/50*cos(3+t)

Get the eBook for only $10!

Now you can take the weightless companion with you anywhere, anytime. Your purchase of this book entitles you to 3 electronic versions for only $10.

This Apress title will prove so indispensible that you'll want to carry it with you everywhere, which is why we are offering the eBook in 3 formats for only $10 if you have already purchased the print book.

Convenient and fully searchable, the PDF version enables you to easily find and copy code—or perform examples by quickly toggling between instructions and applications. The MOBI format is ideal for your Kindle, while the ePUB can be utilized on a variety of mobile devices.

Go to www.apress.com/promo/tendollars to purchase your companion eBook.

Apress®
THE EXPERT'S VOICE™